PEOPLE YOU SHOULD KNOW

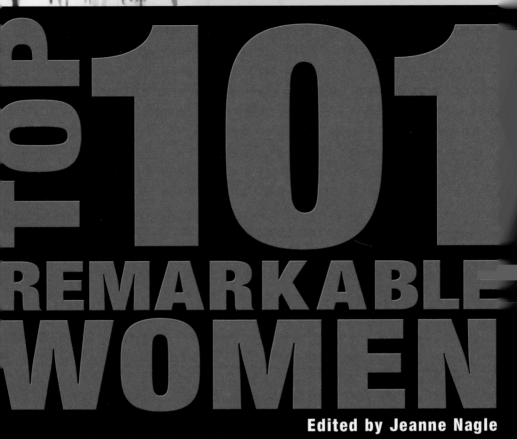

TOP 101 REMARKABLE WOMEN

Edited by Jeanne Nagle

Britannica®
Educational Publishing

IN ASSOCIATION WITH

ROSEN
EDUCATIONAL SERVICES

Published in 2014 by Britannica Educational Publishing (a trademark of Encyclopædia Britannica, Inc.) in association with The Rosen Publishing Group, Inc.
29 East 21st Street, New York, NY 10010

Distributed exclusively by Rosen Publishing.
To see additional Britannica Educational Publishing titles, go to rosenpublishing.com

First Edition

Britannica Educational Publishing
J.E. Luebering: Director, Core Reference Group
Anthony L. Green: Editor, Compton's by Britannica

Rosen Publishing
Hope Lourie Killcoyne: Executive Editor
Jeanne Nagle: Editor
Nelson Sá: Art Director
Brian Garvey: Designer, Cover Design
Cindy Reiman: Photography Manager
Amy Feinberg: Photo Research

Cataloging-in-Publication Data

Top 101 remarkable women/editor, Jeanne Nagle.—First edition.
    pages cm.—(People you should know)
Includes bibliographical references and index.
ISBN 978-1-62275-126-6 (library bound)
1. Women—Biography--Juvenile literature. I. Nagle, Jeanne. II. Title: Top one hundred one remarkable women.
CT3207.T67 2014
920.72—dc23
[B]

2013033326

Manufactured in the United States of America

CONTENTS

8

29

43

95

121

142

INTRODUCTION

The world is filled with fascinating women, each with her own compelling story. Clearly, no single tome can hold all the intricate details of their collective lives. But this book covers many of the most outstanding, influential women from around the globe.

Women of great substance have led countries and driven policy since ancient times. Hatshepsut, the eldest daughter of ancient Egyptian King Thutmose I, wielded unprecedented power for a woman while ruling after her father's death. Another ruler of Egypt, Cleopatra, was the driving force behind the Egyptian throne for twenty-two years.

Centuries later, in England, Elizabeth I overcame in-fighting and political strife to become the queen of England. Her reign is considered a golden age in English history. Another influential monarch in English history is Queen Victoria I, who ruled the United Kingdom for almost sixty-four years.

Other countries around the world have been led by women in the modern age. The first female prime minister in history was Sirimavo Bandaranaike, elected to lead Sri Lanka in 1960. Six years later, Indira Gandhi became the first female prime minister of India. Ireland elected its first female president, Mary Robinson, in 1990, and in 2006, Ellen Johnson-Sirleaf became the first woman to be head of state in an African country when she was elected president of Liberia. While the United States has yet to elect a woman president, former First Lady Hillary Rodham Clinton was named secretary of state during President Barack Obama's administration, after first serving as a United States senator.

There have been many brave women who battled the social norms of their era. In the 1800s, Harriet Tubman fought to see African American men and women treated as equal in American society. Despite being mocked and arrested, Susan B. Anthony spent nearly two-thirds of her life crusading for women's right to vote. Rosa Parks refused to give up her seat to a white man, an act that led to an important event in the U.S. civil rights movement, the Montgomery (Alabama) bus boycott of 1956–57. More recently, Aung San Suu Kyi risked repeated imprisonment fighting for democracy and human rights in Myanmar.

Holding political office isn't the only means by which women have exerted influence. Florence Nightingale, fondly remembered primarily as a nurse, was also a tireless social reformer instrumental in overhauling military medical systems. Influential women of science include Marie Curie, who isolated radium and devoted the later part of her career to uncovering the medical applications of radioactive substances, and Rosalind Franklin, who played a vital role in unraveling the mystery of DNA.

Then there are the women who have left their mark on humankind's collective creative history. Sarah Bernhardt and Marlene Dietrich, for example, are grand dames of stage and screen, respectively. Lucille Ball was not only a wonderful comedic actress but also a shrewd businessperson who became one of the first women to run a major Hollywood production company. Joining Homer in the ranks of great poets of ancient Greece is Sappho, who wrote about love and passion. And a woman, Japanese author Murasaki Shikibu, is credited with having written the world's first novel, *The Tale of Genji*.

The influence of these women and others profiled in this book reverberates throughout the ages. Their leadership, scientific research, and artistic vision have served to enrich, enlighten, and shape modern society. These amazing and influential individuals have given all of us, men and women alike, something to admire and strive for in our own lives.

JANE ADDAMS

(b. 1860–d. 1935)

An early concern for the living conditions of 19th-century factory workers led Jane Addams to assume a pioneering role in the field of social work. She brought cultural and day-care programs to the poor, sought justice for immigrants and blacks, championed labor reform, supported women's suffrage, and helped to train other social workers.

Addams was born on Sept. 6, 1860, in Cedarville, Ill. Her father, John Huy Addams, was a wealthy miller, a state senator, and a friend of Abraham Lincoln. Jane was the youngest of five children. From infancy she suffered from a slight spinal curvature. After graduation from Rockford Seminary (now Rockford College) in Illinois, her health failed, and for two years she was an invalid.

In 1883, Addams went abroad to travel and to study. The hunger and misery she found in the great European cities impressed her more than their famous museums or historic relics. A childhood resolve to live among the poor was confirmed by a stay at Toynbee Hall in London, the world's first social settlement.

In the fall of 1889, she settled with a school friend, Ellen Gates Starr, in a shabby old mansion on the Near West Side of Chicago among tenements and sweatshops. Their neighbors—people of a dozen races—called the place the "old Hull house" after its builder, Charles Hull. So Hull House was adopted as the name for what was to become the most famous social settlement in the United States.

At first the neighbors were suspicious and unfriendly, but they soon saw that Addams's friendliness was sincere and practical. A kindergarten and a day nursery were started. Wealthy people, university professors, students, and business executives contributed time and money to Hull House.

Hull House fed the hungry, nursed the sick, and guided the bewildered immigrant and the wayward child. Addams became a garbage inspector so that she could get the filthy streets cleaned up. She campaigned against the sweatshops and corrupt politicians. She and her

1

Jane Addams, founder of the Hull House.
Fotosearch/Archive Photos/Getty Images

associates at Hull House helped to pass the first factory legislation in Illinois and to establish in Chicago the world's first juvenile court.

Addams became one of the most deeply loved and famous Americans of her time. Universities presented her with honorary degrees. Visitors from all over the world came to see her at Hull House. Crowds in many countries heard her talk about her work.

Addams's best known writings are *Democracy and Social Ethics* (1902), *Newer Ideals of Peace* (1907), *The Spirit of Youth and the City Streets* (1909), *Twenty Years at Hull-House* (1910), *A New Conscience and an Ancient Evil* (1911), and *The Second Twenty Years at Hull-House* (1930).

During World War I, Addams faced bitter criticism when she urged that the issues be settled by negotiation rather than by bloodshed. After the war she continued to spread her ideals as president of the Women's International League for Peace and Freedom. In 1931, she was awarded the Nobel Peace Prize jointly with Dr. Nicholas Murray Butler.

For 46 years Addams managed the settlement. Starr had been forced by ill health to retire about six years before the death of Addams on May 21, 1935. At the time of her death, Hull House had been expanded to cover an entire city block, with buildings centered around a courtyard. In 1961 plans were laid to tear down Hull House to make room for a Chicago campus of the University of Illinois. Despite vehement, worldwide protests against such plans, the properties were sold in 1963.

The original building, however, was preserved as a memorial to Jane Addams. Hull House settlement work has continued in new locations in Chicago.

SUSAN B. ANTHONY

(b. 1820–d. 1906)

For more than half a century Susan B. Anthony fought for women's right to vote. Many people made fun of her. Some insulted her. Nevertheless, she traveled from county to county in New York and other states making speeches and organizing clubs for women's rights. She pleaded her cause with every president from Abraham Lincoln to Theodore Roosevelt.

Susan Bronwell Anthony was born February 1820, in Adams, Mass. Raised in the Quaker tradition, she was a precocious child who learned to read and write at the age of three. After the family moved from Massachusetts to Battensville, N.Y., in 1826, she attended a district school, then a school set up by her father, and finally a boarding school near Philadelphia. In 1839, she took a position in a Quaker seminary in New Rochelle, N.Y. After teaching at a female academy in upstate New York (1846–49), she settled in her family home, in Rochester, New York. There she met many leading abolitionists, including Frederick Douglass, Parker Pillsbury, Wendell Phillips, William Henry Channing, and William Lloyd Garrison.

Anthony was also active in the temperance movement, which was against drinking alcohol, and an ardent abolitionist, meaning she was against slavery. When blacks were given the right to vote by the 15th Amendment, she launched a campaign to extend the same right to women. In 1869, she helped to organize the National Woman Suffrage Association.

In 1890, this group joined the American Woman Suffrage Association to form the National American Woman Suffrage Association. She became the president of the new association in 1892 and held this office until she was 80 years old. In 1872, she voted in the presidential election to test her status as a citizen. For this act she was tried and fined $100,

3

but she refused to pay the fine, declaring that "taxation without representation is tyranny."

At the time when Anthony began her work, women had few legal rights. Today, largely through her efforts and those of her associates, women have opportunities for higher education, the privilege of working at almost any occupation, the right to control their own property and children, the right to hold public office, and the right to vote. She lived to see many of these reforms put into effect. After she died on March 13, 1906, in Rochester, both major political parties endorsed women's suffrage. In 1920, the suffrage amendment to the Constitution was ratified.

AUNG SAN SUU KYI

(b. 1945–)

The leader of the opposition to the ruling military government in Myanmar (formerly Burma), Aung San Suu Kyi brought international attention to the struggle for human rights and the restoration of democracy in her country. An advocate of nonviolent protest, she was under house arrest in Yangon when she was awarded the 1991 Nobel Peace Prize.

Aung San Suu Kyi was born on June 19, 1945, in Rangoon (now Yangon). Her father, Aung San, was regarded as the founder of modern Burma after he negotiated the country's independence from Britain. He was assassinated in 1947. Her mother, Khin Kyi, a prominent diplomat, was named ambassador to India in 1960. After studying in India, Aung San Suu Kyi earned a bachelor's degree at the University of Oxford, where she met her future husband, British scholar Michael Aris. She subsequently worked for the United Nations in New York City and in 1985–86 was a visiting scholar in Southeast Asian studies at Kyoto University in Japan. She returned to Burma in April 1988 to care for her ailing mother, who died later that year.

By the end of 1988, Suu Kyi was heavily involved in the protest movements sweeping the country against the brutal rule of military strongman Ne Win. She initiated a nonviolent struggle for democracy and human rights, helping to form the National League for Democracy (NLD), a political party. In July 1989, the military government of newly named Myanmar placed her under house arrest. The military offered to free her if she agreed to leave Myanmar, but she refused to do so until the country was returned to civilian government. In the 1990 parliamentary elections, the NLD won more than 80 percent of the seats that were contested. The military government ignored the election results, however, and did not allow the new parliament to meet. *Freedom from Fear: And Other Writings*, a collection of her articles and speeches edited by Aris, was published in 1991 following the Nobel Prize announcement. Suu Kyi was eventually freed from house arrest in July 1995.

Despite her release, Suu Kyi was officially barred from leading the NLD, and her movements remained restricted. In 1998, she announced the formation of a representative committee that she declared was the country's legitimate ruling parliament. The military regime once again placed her under house arrest from September 2000 to May 2002.

Following clashes between the NLD and pro-government demonstrators in 2003, the government returned Suu Kyi to house arrest. The international community continued to call for her release. In May 2009, shortly before her sentence was to be completed, an intruder (a U.S. citizen) entered her house compound and spent two nights there. Suu Kyi was arrested and convicted of breaching the terms of her house arrest.

It was widely believed that this conviction was intended to prevent her from participating in the 2010 multiparty parliamentary elections—the first to be held since 1990. Indeed, in 2010, new election laws barred individuals who had been convicted of a crime from participating. They also prohibited anyone who was married to a foreign national (as she was) from running for office. In support of Suu Kyi, the NLD refused to reregister under these new laws (as was required) and was disbanded. In the November 2010 elections, the government parties won an overwhelming majority of legislative seats amid widespread allegations of voter fraud. Six days after the elections, Suu Kyi was released from house arrest. She vowed to continue her opposition to military rule.

Government restrictions on Suu Kyi's activities were further relaxed during 2011. She was allowed to meet with Myanmar's new civilian president as well as the prime minister of Thailand and the U.S. Secretary of State. Meanwhile, rules on political participation were eased, and the NLD was officially reinstated. Suu Kyi was permitted to run for parliament in elections in April 2012. She easily won a seat representing Yangon. Later in 2012, she traveled outside Myanmar for the first time since 1988. On a tour of Europe, Suu Kyi gave the acceptance speech for her 1991 Nobel Prize in Oslo, Norway, and she addressed the British Parliament in London, England.

JANE AUSTEN

(b. 1775–d. 1817)

Through her portrayals of ordinary people in everyday life, Jane Austen gave the genre of the novel its modern character. She began writing at an early age. At 15 she was writing plays and sketches for the amusement of her family, and by the time she was 21 she had begun to write novels that are among the finest in English literature.

Austen was born on Dec. 16, 1775, in the parsonage of Steventon, a village in Hampshire, England. She had six brothers and one sister. Her father, the Reverend George Austen, was a rector of the village. Although she and her sister briefly attended several different schools, Jane was educated mainly by her father, who taught his own children and several pupils who boarded with the family.

Her father retired when Jane was 25. By that time her brothers, two of whom later became admirals, had careers and families of their own. Jane, her sister Cassandra, and their parents went to live in Bath. After the father's death in 1805, the family lived temporarily in Southampton before finally settling in Chawton.

Austen wrote two novels before she was 22. These she later revised and published as *Sense and Sensibility* (1811) and *Pride and Prejudice* (1813). She completed her third novel, *Northanger Abbey*, when she was 27 or 28, but it did not appear in print until after her death. She wrote three more novels in her late 30s: *Mansfield Park* (1814), *Emma* (1816), and *Persuasion* (published together with *Northanger Abbey* in 1818).

Austen wrote of the world she knew. Her novels portray the lives of the gentry and clergy of rural England, and they take place in the country villages and neighborhoods, with an occasional visit to Bath and London. Her world was small, but she saw it clearly and portrayed it with wit and detachment. She described her writing as "the little bit (two inches wide) of ivory on which I work with so fine a brush, as produces little effect after much labor."

Austen died on July 18, 1817, after a long illness. She spent the last weeks of her life in Winchester, near her physician, and is buried in the cathedral there.

LUCILLE BALL

(b. 1911–d. 1989)

On Jan. 19, 1953, Americans sat glued to their television sets as character Lucy Ricardo, played by zany redheaded actress Lucille Ball, gave birth on the situation comedy *I Love Lucy*. The event attracted more viewers than the televised presidential inauguration of Dwight D. Eisenhower the following night. The popularity was a long time in the making for Ball, an established motion-picture actress who found her niche on television playing a wisecracking housewife whose schemes to avoid domestic duties resulted in hilarious misadventures. The program showcased Ball's expertise for timing, physical comedy, and range of characterization.

Lucille Désirée Ball was born on Aug. 6, 1911, in Celoron, near Jamestown, N.Y. Her father died in 1915, and she was raised by her mother and maternal grandparents. Determined to become an actress, Ball left high school at age 15 to enroll in a drama school in New York City, where she was told she lacked talent. Unsuccessful at casting calls, she took jobs as a model under the name Diane Belmont. A poster on which she appeared brought her to the attention of Hollywood studios and won her spots in *Roman Scandals* (1933), *Blood Money* (1933), *Kid Millions* (1934), and other movies.

Ball remained in Hollywood and appeared in increasingly larger roles in a succession of movies—*Carnival* (1935), *Stage Door* (1937), *Room*

Portrait of comedic actress Lucille Ball. Mondadori/Getty Images

Service (1938), and *Five Came Back* (1939). In 1940, she married Cuban bandleader Desi Arnaz, her co-star in the movie *Too Many Girls* (1940). For ten years they conducted separate careers. She won major roles in *The Big Street* (1942) with Henry Fonda, *Du Barry Was a Lady* (1943), *Without Love* (1945), *Ziegfeld Follies* (1946), and *Sorrowful Jones* (1949) and *Fancy Pants* (1950), the last two with Bob Hope. All of her comedies were box-office successes, but they failed to make the most of her wide-ranging talents.

In 1950, Ball and her husband formed Desilu Productions. The company experimented with a radio program before launching the television comedy *I Love Lucy* (1951–56; from 1957 to 1958, hour-long specials were made under the title *The Lucille Ball-Desi Arnaz Show*), which starred the two in roles somewhat mirroring their real lives. *I Love Lucy* was an instant hit and won numerous Emmy Awards. The first television series to be filmed in front of a live studio audience, it also introduced several technical innovations to television broadcasting, notably the use of three cameras to film the program. As the first series to be preserved on high-quality film, it was rerun for decades in more than 70 countries.

Desilu later acquired RKO Pictures and began producing other shows for television. Ball and Arnaz had a son and a daughter together and divorced in 1960. Two years later she bought him out to become president of Desilu, making her the only woman at that time to lead a major Hollywood production company. Ball married former talk-show host Gary Morton in 1961.

Ball starred on Broadway in *Wildcat* (1961) before returning to television in *The Lucy Show* (1962–68). She resumed movie work with *Yours, Mine and Ours* (1968) and *Mame* (1974). In 1967, Ball sold Desilu for a substantial profit and formed her own company, Lucille Ball Productions, which produced her third television series, *Here's Lucy* (1968–74). She played a Manhattan bag lady in the dramatic television film *Stone Pillow* (1985). Her fourth television series, *Life with Lucy*, aired for two months in 1986.

Days after undergoing open-heart surgery, Ball died on April 26, 1989, in Los Angeles, Calif. Her memoir, *Love, Lucy,* was written in the early 1960s but published posthumously in 1996.

SIRIMAVO R.D. BANDARANAIKE

(b. 1916–d. 2000)

Upon her party's victory in the 1960 Ceylon general election, Sirimavo R.D. Bandaranaike became the world's first woman prime minister. She left office in 1965 but returned to serve two more terms (1970–77, 1994–2000) as prime minister. The family she founded with her late husband, S.W.R.D. Bandaranaike, rose to great prominence in Sri Lankan politics.

She was born Sirimavo Ratwatte on April 17, 1916, near Kandy, Ceylon (now Sri Lanka). Her family was wealthy, and she was educated in convent schools. In 1940, she married S.W.R.D. Bandaranaike, a member of Ceylon's cabinet and prime minister from 1956 to 1959. They had three children.

Bandaranaike was not politically active until 1959, when her husband was assassinated. She led the nationalist Sri Lanka Freedom Party (SLFP) to win the parliamentary elections of July 1960 and was named prime minister to succeed her husband's replacement. She carried on her husband's program of socialist economic policies, neutrality in international relations, and the active encouragement of Buddhism and Sinhala, the religion and language of the Sinhalese, who made up a majority of the population. To reduce foreign influence in Ceylon, which was ruled by Britain until 1948, Bandaranaike replaced English with Sinhalese as the nation's official language. Her government nationalized various economic enterprises and mission schools. By 1964, a deepening economic crisis and the SLFP's coalition with the Marxist Lanka Sama Samaja Party (Ceylon Socialist Party) had eroded popular support for her government, which was soundly defeated in the general election of March 1965.

In 1970, however, her socialist coalition, the United Front, regained power, and as prime minister Bandaranaike pursued more radical policies. Her government further restricted free enterprise, nationalized industries, carried out land reforms, and declared a new constitution that created an executive presidency and made Ceylon into a republic named Sri Lanka. While reducing inequalities of wealth, Bandaranaike's socialist policies had once again caused economic stagnation, and her government's support of Buddhism and the Sinhalese language had helped alienate the country's large Tamil minority. The failure to deal with ethnic rivalries and economic distress led, in the election of July 1977, to the SLFP's retaining only eight of the 168 seats in the National Assembly, and Bandaranaike was replaced as prime minister.

In 1980, the Sri Lanka parliament stripped her of her political rights and barred her from political office, but in 1986, President J.R. Jayawardene granted her a pardon that restored her rights. She ran unsuccessfully as the SLFP's candidate for president in 1988, and after regaining a seat in parliament in 1989, she became the leader of the opposition.

When Bandaranaike's daughter, Chandrika Bandaranaike Kumaratunga, became prime minister in 1994, she appointed her mother to serve as prime minister in her new government, which mounted a major military campaign against Tamil separatists in 1995.

Failing health forced Bandaranaike to resign her post in August 2000. Shortly after voting in the parliamentary elections, she suffered a heart attack and died on October 10 of that year, in Colombo.

GERTRUDE BELL

(b. 1868–d. 1926)

English traveler and writer Gertrude Bell worked as an administrator in Arabia. She played a principal part in the establishment of the Hāshimite Dynasty in Baghdad.

Gertrude Margaret Lowthian Bell was born on July 14, 1868, in Durham, England. Her time studying at Oxford University was followed by some time spent in Tehrān, where her uncle Sir Frank Lascelles was British minister. In 1899, after first returning to England and Europe, she embarked on the career of Arabian activities that made her famous.

Bell visited Palestine and Syria and was often back in the Middle East during the next decade, extending her travels to Asia Minor. But her heart was set on an Arabian journey, which she began in 1913, being the second woman (after Lady Anne Blunt) to visit Ha'il, where she was not favorably received.

Bell never wrote a full account of this journey, though her literary output during the 20 years preceding World War I had been considerable, including *Safar Nameh* (1894), *Poems from the Divan of Hafiz* (1897), *The Desert and the Sown* (1907), *The Thousand and One Churches* (1909), and *Amurath to Amurath* (1911). Her vast correspondence was published in an edited form in two volumes by her stepmother in 1927.

Perhaps her greatest work was a masterly official report on the administration of Mesopotamia during the difficult period between the Armistice of 1918 and the Iraq rebellion of 1920. After a short period of war work in England and France, Bell plunged into Middle East politics, mainly in Mesopotamia. She helped place the Hāshimite ruler Fayṣal I on the throne of Iraq in 1921.

The last three years of Bell's life were devoted to the creation of an archaeological museum in Baghdad. She insisted that antiquities excavated should stay in the country of their origin, thereby ensuring that the National Museum of Iraq would possess a splendid collection of Iraq's own antiquities. Facing ill health and profound loneliness, Bell took a fatal dose of sleeping pills and died July 12, 1926, in Baghdad.

SARAH BERNHARDT

(b. 1844–d. 1923)

A celebrated French actress, Sarah Bernhardt is one of the best-known figures in the history of the stage. She performed throughout Europe and the United States.

She was born Henriette Rosine Bernard on Oct. 22 or 23 (the date is uncertain), 1844, in Paris, France. (She later changed her name for the stage.) She was the illegitimate daughter of Julie Bernard, a Dutch courtesan who had established herself in Paris (the identity of her father is uncertain). As the presence of a baby interfered with her mother's life, Sarah was brought up at first in a pension and later in a convent. A difficult, willful child of delicate health, she wanted to become a nun, but one of her mother's lovers, the duke de Morny, Napoleon III's half brother, decided that she should be an actress.

At the age of 16 she entered the Conservatoire, the government-sponsored school of acting, and two years later she made her debut at the Comédie Française. In 1866, she signed a contract with the Odéon Theatre and, during six years of intensive work with a theater company there, gradually established her reputation. Bernhardt experienced her first theatrical triumph at age 25, when she gave such a fine performance that she was asked to repeat it before Napoleon III, emperor of France. During the Franco-German War in 1870, she organized a military hospital in the Odéon Theatre.

In 1872, Bernhardt left the Odéon and returned to the Comédie-Française. She played Desdemona in Shakespeare's *Othello* in 1878, and, when the Comédie-Française appeared in London in 1879, Bernhardt played in the second act of *Phèdre* and achieved another triumph. She had now reached the head of her profession, and an international career lay before her. Bernhardt had become an expressive actress with a wide emotional range who was capable of great subtlety in her interpretations. Her grace, beauty, and charisma gave her a commanding stage presence, and the impact of her unique voice was reinforced by the purity of her diction. Her career was also helped by her relentless self-promotion and her unconventional behavior both on and off the stage.

In 1880, Bernhardt formed a traveling company and soon became an international idol. She appeared regularly in England but also performed on the Continent and in the United States, Canada, Australia, and South America. She developed a flamboyant style of acting, relying on lavish decors, exotic costumes, and pantomime actions.

In 1905, she injured her right knee when she jumped off a parapet. By 1915, gangrene had set in, and the leg was amputated. This did not prevent her from visiting soldiers at the front during World War I.

In 1916, Bernhardt began her last tour of the United States, and her indomitable spirit sustained her during 18 grueling months on the road. In November 1918, she arrived back in France but soon set out on another European tour, playing parts she could act while seated. New roles were provided for her by the playwrights Louis Verneuil, Maurice Rostand, and

Sacha Guitry. She collapsed during the dress rehearsal of a Guitry play, and despite a brief recovery, died on March 26, 1923, in her home in Paris.

ELIZABETH BLACKWELL

(b. 1821–d. 1910)

W hen Elizabeth Blackwell was graduated as a doctor of medicine in 1849, she became the first woman doctor in the United States. Her enrollment in the Medical Register of the United Kingdom in 1859 made her Europe's first modern woman doctor.

Elizabeth Blackwell was born on Feb. 3, 1821, in Bristol, England. She was one of nine children of Samuel Blackwell, a prosperous sugar refiner. The Blackwells immigrated to New York City in 1832. There the family was active in the abolitionist movement. Their refinery unfortunately did not prosper, and in 1838, they moved to Cincinnati, Ohio. Samuel Blackwell died a few months after the move. The need for the boys to find work and the girls to start school did not prevent the Blackwells from aiding escaped slaves or from participating in intellectual movements.

It was in 1844 that slight, yellow-haired Elizabeth Blackwell determined to become a doctor. Because no medical school would admit her, she studied privately with doctors in the South and in Philadelphia. In 1847, the Geneva Medical School of western New York accepted her. The acceptance evoked a storm of ridicule and criticism, but in spite of slights and embarrassments Elizabeth pursued her studies. In 1849, she was graduated at the head of her class.

Paris then was the foremost medical center. Blackwell journeyed there to undertake advanced studies, but Paris doctors proved as intolerant as their American colleagues. They would not permit her to study as a doctor. She was forced to enter a large maternity hospital as a student midwife. There she contracted an infection that caused her to lose her sight in one eye. After convalescence, she went to London, where she was permitted to continue her studies.

On her return to New York City in 1850, Blackwell was not permitted to practice in any hospital. Dr. Blackwell fought for her own and other women's rights to learn and practice. She started the New York Infirmary for Women and Children, aided by her sister Emily and other women who became doctors and by several tolerant Quakers. Her leadership in meeting the medical problems presented by the Civil War won her recognition. With her sister she opened a medical college for women in her hospital.

Blackwell wrote and lectured. A series of lectures which she delivered in England in 1859 brought her recognition in Britain. After the Civil War she settled in England. Her work and her friendship with Florence Nightingale and other intellectual leaders of the day opened the way for English women to enter the field of medicine.

Blackwell's lectures and books dealt largely with social hygiene and with preventive medicine. She died on May 31, 1910, at her home in Hastings, England.

BRONTË SISTERS

Charlotte Brontë (b. 1816–d. 1855)
Emily Brontë (b. 1818–d. 1848)
Anne Brontë (b. 1820–d. 1849)

The bleak, lonely moors of Yorkshire in England were the setting for two great novels of the 19th century, Charlotte Brontë's *Jane Eyre* and Emily Brontë's *Wuthering Heights*. Their youngest sister, Anne, was also a talented novelist, and her books have the same haunting quality.

The Brontë sisters were born in Yorkshire, England. Charlotte, the eldest, was born in 1816. Emily was born in 1818 and Anne in 1820. Their father was Patrick Brontë, a Church of England priest. Irish-born, he had changed his name from the more commonplace Brunty. After serving in several parishes he moved with his wife, Maria Branwell Brontë, and their six small children to Haworth in Yorkshire in 1820. Soon after, Mrs. Brontë and the two eldest children died, leaving the father to care for the remaining three girls and a boy.

Left to themselves, the children wrote and told stories and walked over the moors. They grew up largely self-educated. Branwell showed some talent for drawing. The girls determined to earn money for his art

Portrait of (left to right) *Anne, Emily, and Charlotte Brontë, painted by their brother, Branwell.* The Bridgeman Art Library/Getty Images

education. They took positions as teachers and governesses, but they were unhappy at being separated and away from Haworth.

To keep the family together, Charlotte planned to keep a school for girls at Haworth. She and Emily went to Brussels to learn foreign languages and school management. In 1844, using a small inheritance from an aunt, they prepared to open classes. Although they advertised, they received no pupils.

The failure of their venture left all the children at home. Charlotte again sought a way to help the family. She had found some of Emily's poems, written secretly, and realized their merit. She convinced her sisters they should publish a joint book of poems. In 1846, the girls brought out at their own expense *Poems by Currer, Ellis, and Acton Bell.*

They chose masculine pen names but retained their own initials. Although critics liked the poems, only two volumes were sold.

As children they had all written many stories. Charlotte, as a young girl, alone filled 22 volumes, each with 60 to 100 pages of minute handwriting. Again they turned to writing as a source of income. By 1847, Charlotte had written *The Professor*; Emily, *Wuthering Heights*; and Anne, *Agnes Grey*. After much difficulty Anne and Emily found a publisher, but Charlotte's book was not wanted. (It was not published until 1859.) However, one publisher expressed an interest in seeing more of her work. *Jane Eyre* was already started, and she hurriedly finished it. It was accepted at once; thus each of the sisters had a book published in 1847.

Jane Eyre was immediately successful; the other two did not fare so well. Critics were hostile to *Wuthering Heights*. They said it was too wild, too animal-like. But silent, reserved Emily had put all her deep feelings into the book, and gradually it came to be considered one of the finest novels in the English language. Emily lived only a short while after the publication of her book, and Anne died in 1849.

Charlotte published *Shirley* in 1849, and *Villette* in 1853. She was acclaimed by London literary society, especially by William Makepeace Thackeray. In 1854, she married her father's assistant, Arthur Bell Nicholls. But only a year later, she died of tuberculosis, as her sisters had.

GRO HARLEM BRUNDTLAND

(b. 1939–)

Norwegian politician Gro Harlem Brundtland was the first woman prime minister of Norway and one of the most influential world figures on environmental issues. From 1998 to 2003, she was director general of the World Health Organization, tackling global pandemics such as AIDS and SARS.

Brundtland was born on April 20, 1939, in Oslo, Norway. She received a medical degree from the University of Oslo in 1963 and a master's degree in public health from Harvard University in 1965. She then worked as a public health officer in Oslo. A member of the Labor Party, she was minister of the environment from 1974 to 1979, and she was first elected to parliament in 1977. In 1975, she was elected deputy leader of the party, and in 1981, its leader.

Brundtland was appointed prime minister in 1981, but she served for only nine months because her Labor lost the elections held later that year. She returned as prime minister from 1986 to 1989, and again from 1990 to 1996.

Brundtland became identified with public health and environmental issues and is credited with securing better educational and economic opportunities for women in Norway. In 1983, she became chair of the United Nations World Commission on Environment and Development, which eventually led to the first Earth Summit.

ANNIE JUMP CANNON

(b. 1863–d. 1941)

Known as the "census taker of the sky," American astronomer Annie Jump Cannon developed the Harvard system of classifying stars. Her method involved studying the spectra, or properties of light, emitted by the stars.

Annie Jump Cannon was born in Dover, Delaware, on Dec. 11, 1863. After attending Wellesley and Radcliffe colleges, she joined the staff of the Harvard College Observatory and worked there for the rest of her life.

Using her system of spectral classification by surface temperature, she demonstrated that the vast majority of stars can be grouped into only a few types and those types can be arranged into a continuous series. She measured and classified spectra for more than 225,300 stars of ninth magnitude or brighter. Her work was published in the *Henry Draper Catalogue* from 1918 to 1924.

In addition to classifying thousands of stars, Cannon also discovered more than 300 variable stars and five novas. The first woman ever awarded an honorary doctorate by Oxford University, Cannon continued her research until her death at Cambridge, Mass., on April 13, 1941.

MARY CASSATT

(b. 1844–d. 1926)

American painter and printmaker Mary Cassatt exhibited her works with those of the Impressionists in France. She persuaded many of her wealthy American friends to buy Impressionist art, thus influencing American taste in painting.

Cassatt was born in Allegheny City (now a part of Pittsburgh), Pa., on May 22, 1844. She was the daughter of a banker and lived in Europe for five years as a young girl. She was tutored privately in art in Philadelphia and attended the Pennsylvania Academy of the Fine Arts in 1861–65, but she preferred a less academic approach, and in 1866, traveled to Europe to study with such European painters as Jean-Léon Gérôme and Thomas Couture.

Cassatt's first major showing was at the Paris Salon of 1872. Her work was noticed by painter Edgar Degas when it was shown in the 1874 Salon exhibit. Degas did not usually befriend women, but he asked Cassatt to join the Impressionists—painters who used color and brush-strokes in new ways—and the two became close friends. Cassatt's work was included in Impressionist exhibits in 1879, 1880, 1881, and 1886.

Her paintings were first shown on their own in Paris in 1891. Degas's influence on Cassatt is evident in her skillful drawing and in the uncentered, casual arrangement of her subjects. But her drawing is less cluttered and more precise than that of Degas. After an exhibition of Japanese prints in Paris in 1890, she began to emphasize line and pattern rather than form and displayed a series of ten colored prints, or etchings, that were especially masterful.

She is most famous for her pictures of mothers caring for small children, as in *The Bath*, painted about 1892.

Cassatt was important not only for the art she created, but also for the art she taught people to appreciate. She collected Impressionist paintings herself and encouraged her wealthy associates to do the same, speeding the acceptance of Impressionism in America.

Like her friend Degas, Cassatt developed eye trouble. Her sight began to fail soon after 1900, and by 1914, she stopped painting. She died, nearly blind, on June 14, 1926, in Château de Beaufresne, near Paris.

CATHERINE II

(b. 1729–d. 1796)

Princess Sophie Auguste Friederike of Anhalt-Zerbst, was an obscure German princess who became one of the most powerful women in history as Catherine II, also known as Catherine the Great, empress of Russia. She expanded the territory of Russia and was known for her brilliant court, to which the greatest minds of Europe were drawn.

She was born at Stettin in the Prussian province of Pomerania (now Szczecin, Poland) on May 2, 1729 (April 21 according to the calendar in use at the time). Early in 1744, when she was almost 15, Sophie was presented to Empress Elizabeth of Russia, who was seeking a wife for her 16-year-old nephew, the Grand Duke Peter, heir to the Russian throne. She was received into the Russian Orthodox Church and rechristened Catherine. Peter and Catherine were married in 1745. Their first child, who became Czar Paul I, was born in 1754. In 1757, she had a daughter, Anne, who died in 1758. A son, Alexei, was born in 1762.

When Empress Elizabeth died in January 1762, Peter became Czar Peter III. His childish behavior and preference for German ways and the Lutheran religion soon made him unpopular. By accepting Russian customs as her own, Catherine had gained many supporters, including members of the army. In early July 1762, the army arrested Peter, and Catherine was declared empress. Peter died while in custody.

For years Catherine had studied the works of such French Enlightenment thinkers as Charles de Montesquieu, Denis Diderot, and Voltaire. Her enthusiasm for Western culture led to the flourishing of scholarship, book publishing, journalism, architecture, and the theater. Catherine herself wrote articles and plays. She sponsored the first school for girls in Russia and established a system of elementary schools. After the French Revolution, however, she became critical of liberal attitudes.

Although Catherine was eager to be considered progressive, many of her social policies were reactionary. Between 1767 and 1768, she sponsored a commission to codify Russian laws, only to cancel the project when the delegates produced no results. After a peasant rebellion in 1773–74, she instituted a new system of local government that strengthened the power of the local landlords. Under her Charter to the Nobility of 1785, the landlord's control over peasants and serfs became stronger than ever before.

Catherine fought two wars with Turkey, from 1768 to 1774 and from 1787 to 1792. As a result, Russia won part of the northern Black Sea coast, the Crimean peninsula, and navigation rights in Turkish waters. She also joined with Prussia and Austria in partitioning Poland in 1772, 1793, and 1795. She was extremely ambitious and hoped to conquer even more territory, but these plans were not realized by the time she died on Nov. 17, 1796, in Tsarskoye Selo (now Pushkin), near St. Petersburg, Russia.

VIOLETA BARRIOS DE CHAMORRO

(b. 1929–)

Political leader and newspaper publisher Violeta Barrios de Chamorro was catapulted into politics after the assassination of her husband, Pedro Joaquín Chamorro Cardenal. She served as president of Nicaragua in the 1990s.

She was born Violeta Barrios Torres on Oct. 18, 1929 in Rivas, Nicaragua, into a wealthy family. received much of her early education in the U.S. states of Texas and Virginia. In 1950, shortly after the death of her father, she returned to Nicaragua, where she married Pedro Joaquim Chamorro Cardenal, editor of the newspaper *La Prensa*, which was often critical of the Somoza family dictatorship. The Chamorros were forced into exile in 1957 and lived in Costa Rica for several years before returning to Nicaragua after the Somoza government declared an amnesty.

On January 10, 1978, Pedro Chamorro, who had continued to criticize the Somozas and had been imprisoned several times during the 1960s and '70s, was assassinated. His death helped to spark a revolution, led by the Sandinista National Liberation Front, which toppled the government of Anastasio Somoza Debayle in July 1979. A member of the Sandinista ruling junta (military-led government) in 1979–80, Violeta Chamorro soon became disillusioned with the Sandinistas' Marxist policies, and later she became an outspoken foe. She took over *La Prensa*, which was frequently shut down during the 1980s and was banned completely for a period in 1986–87.

During the 1980s, Chamorro was accused by the Sandinistas of accepting money from the United States Central Intelligence Agency, which was then providing support to opposition groups and directing the Contra rebels in their guerrilla war against the Sandinista government.

An end to the guerrilla war was negotiated in the late 1980s, and free elections were scheduled for 1990. Chamorro, drafted as the presidential candidate of the National Opposition Union (Unión Nacional Opositor; UNO) alliance, won a surprisingly easy victory over President Daniel Ortega Saavedra, head of the Sandinistas. She was inaugurated on April 25, 1990, becoming Central America's first woman president.

During her presidency, Chamorro reversed a number of Sandinista policies. Several state-owned industries were privatized, censorship was lifted, and the size of the army was reduced. At the same time, she retained a number of Sandinistas in the government and attempted to reconcile the country's various political factions. Many credit her conciliatory policies with helping to maintain the fragile peace that had been negotiated. Barred from running for a second term, she retired from politics after her term ended in January 1997.

COCO CHANEL

(b. 1883–d. 1971)

French fashion designer Coco Chanel ruled over Parisian haute couture for almost six decades. Her elegantly casual designs inspired women of fashion to abandon the complicated, uncomfortable clothes—such as petticoats and corsets—that were prevalent in 19th-century dress. Among her now-classic innovations were the Chanel suit, costume jewelry, and the "little black dress."

She was born Gabrielle Bonheur Chanel on Aug. 19, 1883, in Saumur, France. Her mother died when she was young, and her father abandoned her to an orphanage. After a brief stint as a shop-girl, Chanel worked for a few years as a café singer. She later became associated with a series of wealthy men and in 1913, with financial assistance from one of them, opened a tiny millinery (hat) shop in Deauville, where she

Fashion icon and successful businessperson Coco Chanel. Lipnitzki/Roger Viollet/Getty Images

also sold simple sportswear, such as jersey sweaters. Within five years her original use of jersey fabric to create a "poor girl" look had attracted the attention of influential wealthy women.

Faithful to the belief that "luxury must be comfortable, otherwise it is not luxury," Chanel's designs stressed simplicity and comfort and revolutionized the fashion industry. By the late 1920s, the Chanel industries employed 3,500 people and included a couture house, a textile business, perfume laboratories, and a workshop for costume jewelry.

The financial basis of her empire was Chanel No. 5, the successful perfume she introduced in 1922 with the help of Ernst Beaux, one of the most talented perfume creators in France. It has been said that the perfume got its name from the series of scents that Beaux created for Chanel to sample—she chose the fifth, a combination of jasmine and several other floral scents that was more complex and mysterious than the single-scented perfumes then on the market. That Chanel was the first major fashion designer to introduce a perfume and that she replaced the typical perfume packaging with a simple and sleek bottle also added to the scent's success. Unfortunately, her partnerships with businessmen Théophile Bader and Pierre Wertheimer, who promised to help her market her fragrance in exchange for a share of the profits, meant that she received only 10 percent of its royalties before World War II and only 2 percent afterward. Despite enacting a series of lawsuits, Chanel failed to regain control of her signature fragrance.

Chanel closed her couture house in 1939 with the outbreak of World War II but returned in 1954 to introduce her highly copied suit design, a collarless, braid-trimmed cardigan jacket with a graceful skirt. She also introduced bell-bottomed pants and other innovations, while always retaining a clean, classic look.

Chanel died on Jan. 10, 1971, in Paris. After her death, her couture house was led by a series of different designers. This situation stabilized in 1983, when Karl Lagerfeld became chief designer.

CHRISTINA

(b. 1626–d. 1689)

One of the wittiest and most learned women of her time, Christina stunned all of Europe by abdicating, or stepping down from, her throne as the queen of Sweden. She then made attempts, without any success, to gain the crowns of Naples and Poland.

Christina was born on Dec. 8, 1626, in Stockholm to King Gustavus II Adolphus. She became queen-elect before age 6. She was crowned in 1644 and played an important role in ending the Thirty Years' War. When she gave up the crown after 10 years, Christina said she did it because she was not strong enough to rule. The real reasons were her distaste for marriage, urged by her councilors to provide an heir to the throne, and her secret conversion to Roman Catholicism, prohibited in Sweden.

She went to Rome in 1654, where she became well known. Missing the activity of ruling, Christina negotiated with the chief minister of France and the duke of Modena to seize Naples and intended to become its queen. But the scheme collapsed in 1657. Ten years later she attempted to gain the crown of Poland. She failed again and returned to Rome, where she became active in church politics. She died on April 19, 1689, in Rome, leaving behind a vast collection of artwork and institutions for culture and education.

CHRISTINE DE PISAN

(b. 1364–d. 1430)

French poet and author Christine de Pisan produced diverse writings during her lifetime. These include numerous poems of courtly love, a biography of Charles V of France, and several works championing women.

Christine de Pisan was born in 1364 in Venice (which is now part of Italy). Her Italian father served as astrologer to Charles V, and she spent a pleasant childhood at the French court. At age 15 she married Etienne de Castel, who became court secretary. When he died 10 years later, she began writing in order to support herself and her three young children.

Her first poems, about lost love written to the memory of her husband, were successful, so she continued writing in the various popular poetry forms of her day. In all, she wrote 10 volumes in verse, including *L'Épistre au Dieu d'amours* (1399; "Letter to the God of Loves"), in which she defended women against the satire of Jean de Meung's 13th-century poem *Roman de la rose*. In her lifetime Christine achieved much renown and gained the support of such patrons as Louis I, the Duke de Berry, Philip II the Bold of Burgundy, Queen Isabella of Bavaria, and, in England, the 4th Earl of Salisbury.

Christine also wrote numerous prose works, which reveal her remarkable depth of knowledge. *Le Livre de la cité des dames* (1405; The Book of the City of Ladies) displays women known for their heroism and virtue. The sequel, *Le Livre des trois vertus* (1405; "Book of Three Virtues"), classifies women's roles in medieval society and provides moral instructions for women in the different social classes. She tells the story of her life through allegory in *L'Avision de Christine* (1405). Her *Le Livre des fais et bonnes meurs du sage roy Charles V* (1404; "Book of the Deeds and Good Morals of the Wise King Charles V") is a first-hand account of Charles V and his court.

After the defeat of the French at the Battle of Agincourt in 1415, Christine retired to a convent. Her last work, *Le Ditié de Jehanne d'Arc*, which she wrote in 1429, was inspired by the early victories of Joan of Arc. It is the only such French-language work written during Joan's lifetime. Christine died in about 1430.

CIXI

(b. 1835–d. 1908)

Known in the West as the Empress Dowager, Cixi (or Tz'u-hsi) dominated the political life of China for nearly 50 years. As ruler acting for child emperors, she and her cohorts brought a measure of stability to their country. But under her, the government was dishonest and did not make changes that were needed to benefit the people. This eventually led to the end of the Qing Dynasty, which ruled from 1644 to 1911–12, and a revolution.

Cixi was born in Beijing on Nov. 29, 1835. She became a consort of the seventh emperor of the Qing Dynasty, known as the Xianfeng emperor, who ruled from 1850 to 1861. (Qing emperors are known by their reign name, not their personal name.) Cixi bore the emperor's only son. When this son himself became emperor in 1861, as the Tongzhi emperor, he was only 6. Cixi and another former consort became coregents along with a brother of the former emperor. Under this three-way rule the Taiping Rebellion was ended. Other disturbances were put down, and some modernization was brought to China.

Cixi gradually increased her power within the ruling coalition, and even when the emperor matured she continued to control the government. After the young emperor's untimely death, she saw to it that her 3-year-old nephew (whom she had adopted) was named as heir, though this violated succession law. Thus the two empress dowagers continued acting as regents for the new ruler, who was known as the Guangxu emperor. The other dowager died—presumably murdered—in 1881, and Cixi ruled alone. From 1889 to 1898, she lived in apparent retirement in the summer palace.

The new emperor's attempts at reform after losing the Sino-Japanese War (1894–95), however, brought her back into action—determined to stave off any changes. In 1899, she backed the officials promoting the Boxer Rebellion. After China's defeat at the hand of foreign troops, she fled the capital and accepted humiliating peace terms. She returned in 1902 and belatedly tried to implement the reforms she had once opposed.

Cixi died on Nov. 15, 1908, in Beijing; it was then announced that the Guangxu emperor had died the day before. (In 2008, Chinese researchers and police officials confirmed that the Guangxu emperor he had been poisoned with arsenic; presumably, Cixi had ordered him killed.)

Portrait of the Empress Dowager Cixi of the Qing Dynasty, China. Keren Su/China Span/ Getty Images

Cixi had chosen as his successor her 3-year-old grandnephew. The boy was forced from the throne four years later, making him the last Chinese emperor.

CLEOPATRA

(b. 69 BCE–d. 30 BCE)

One of the most fascinating women of all time was Cleopatra VII, queen of Egypt. She had great intelligence and beauty, and she used both to further Egypt's political aims.

Cleopatra was of Greek heritage and culture, one of the Ptolemy line set on the throne of Egypt after the conquest of Alexander the Great. Her father, Ptolemy XII, named her and his elder son, Ptolemy, joint rulers. Cleopatra came to the throne in 51 BCE. Three years later young Ptolemy's supporters had Cleopatra driven into exile.

In 48 BCE Caesar appeared in Egypt in pursuit of his rival, Pompey. When Cleopatra heard that Caesar was in the palace in Alexandria, she had one of her attendants carry her to him, rolled up in a rug offered as a gift. Captivated by her charm, the 52-year-old Roman helped her regain her throne. Ptolemy XIII was drowned, and Caesar made Cleopatra's younger brother, Ptolemy XIV, joint ruler with her.

Cleopatra bore Caesar a son, called Caesarion, meaning "little Caesar." When Caesar returned to Rome, she followed him with their baby and lived in Caesar's villa, where he visited her constantly. After Caesar was assassinated in 44 BCE, Cleopatra returned to Egypt. Soon after, Ptolemy XIV died, perhaps poisoned by Cleopatra, and the queen named her son Caesarion co-ruler with her as Ptolemy Caesar.

Civil war followed Caesar's assassination, and the Roman Empire was divided. Mark Antony, as ruler of the eastern empire, summoned Cleopatra to Tarsus, in Asia Minor, to answer charges that she had aided his enemies. The queen arrived, dressed as Venus, on a magnificent river barge. She welcomed Antony with feasting and entertainment. Fascinated by her, he followed her to Alexandria.

After a festive winter with Cleopatra, Antony returned to Rome. He married Octavia, sister of Octavian (later called Augustus), though he still loved Cleopatra, who had borne him twins. When he went east again, in an expedition against the Parthians, he sent for her and they were married.

Octavian was furious and declared war on Cleopatra. Antony and Cleopatra assembled 500 ships. Octavian blockaded them off the west coast of Greece, and the famous 31 BCE Battle of Actium followed. Cleopatra slipped through the blockade and Antony followed her, but his fleet surrendered.

The next year Octavian reached Alexandria and again defeated Antony. Cleopatra took refuge in the mausoleum she had had built for herself. Antony, informed that Cleopatra was dead, stabbed himself.

Soon another messenger arrived, saying Cleopatra still lived. Antony insisted on being carried to her and died in her arms. Later Cleopatra committed suicide—tradition says by the bite of a poisonous asp.

HILLARY RODHAM CLINTON

(b. 1947–)

In 2000, former first lady Hillary Rodham Clinton captured a seat in the U.S. Senate. She later served as secretary of state in the administration of President Barack Obama.

Hillary Diane Rodham was born in Chicago on Oct. 26, 1947. She grew up in Park Ridge, Ill. Influenced by her parents, she was a Republican in her youth. Her political views changed while she studied political science at Wellesley College in Massachusetts, and she became a Democrat. After graduating in 1969, Rodham entered Yale Law School. There she developed a strong interest in family law and issues affecting children.

Although she met Bill Clinton at Yale, they took separate paths after graduation in 1973. He returned to his native Arkansas, and she stayed in the East to work for the Children's Defense Fund. In 1974, Rodham moved to Arkansas, where she taught at the University Of Arkansas School Of Law. She married Bill Clinton in

U.S. Secretary of State Hillary Clinton, arriving for a meeting with the president of Croatia in 2012. Hrvoje Polan/AFP/Getty Images

29

1975 and joined a prominent law firm in Little Rock, later becoming a partner. The couple's only child, Chelsea, was born in 1980.

While Bill Clinton served as governor of Arkansas (1978–80, 1982–90), Hillary Clinton worked on programs that aided children and the disadvantaged and maintained a successful law practice. She served on the boards of several high-profile corporations and was twice named one of the nation's 100 most influential lawyers (1988, 1991) by the *National Law Journal*. She also served as chair of the Arkansas Education Standards Committee and founded the Arkansas Advocates for Children and Families. She was named Arkansas Woman of the Year in 1983 and Arkansas Young Mother of the Year in 1984.

Clinton played a crucial role in her husband's 1992 presidential campaign. She greeted voters, gave speeches, and was one of his chief advisers. As First Lady, she was appointed to head a task force to devise a national health care policy. She appeared before congressional committees to promote the findings of the task force, winning mostly favorable comments for her expertise on the subject.

Hillary Clinton remained a controversial figure throughout her time in the White House. Her investment in Whitewater, a real estate development in Arkansas, and other business dealings came under investigation. She also received criticism for her involvement in legal maneuvering by the White House during the Whitewater investigation. In 1998, she was thrust into the spotlight again when the president's affair with White House intern Monica Lewinsky was revealed. The First Lady stood by her husband publicly during the scandal and subsequent impeachment.

In 1999, Hillary launched her candidacy for a U.S. Senate seat from New York. After a bitter contest, she defeated Republican Rick Lazio in the 2000 election. As senator, she continued to push for health care reform and remained an advocate for children. She was easily re-elected in 2006.

The next year Hillary announced that she would seek the Democratic presidential nomination for 2008. Considered the early frontrunner, she spent months locked in a tight contest with Senator Barack Obama. Obama eventually secured the nomination and went on to be elected president. He appointed Hillary to serve as secretary of state; she was easily confirmed by the Senate in January 2009.

Clinton's tenure as secretary of state was widely praised for improving U.S. foreign relationships. She resigned from her post in 2013 and was replaced by former Massachusetts senator John Kerry.

COLETTE

(b. 1873–d. 1954)

An outstanding French woman writer of the first half of the 20th century, she called herself, simply, Colette. She would describe soup as tasting like "a badly swept hayloft," or a hot water bottle as being "soft to the feet like a live animal's tummy?" She managed to describe sights, sounds, tastes, smells, and feelings in unique ways that allow a reader almost to experience them.

Sidonie Gabrielle Colette was born on January 28, 1873, in rural Burgundy, France. Colette was a star pupil in school, and, when at 20 she married Henri Gauthier-Villars, they worked together on four novels about a girl named Claudine. The character was based on Colette herself. These novels, published between 1900 and 1903, were very successful, and Colette proceeded to write more stories, often about animals.

After her divorce in 1906, Colette became a music hall actress; yet she managed to publish at least one novel a year. In 1912, she married Henry de Jouvenel, editor of the newspaper *Le Matin*, for which she wrote drama reviews and short stories. During World War I, Colette served as a nurse and converted her husband's estate into a hospital.

Colette is best known for her novels, which include *Chéri, Mitsou*, and *The Vagabond*. Her work combines a strong point of view with realistic details. She often wrote of love—particularly from the female viewpoint—but never stopped including clear descriptions of settings. Such writing produced an effect both sophisticated and natural. Her skill earned her honors rarely given to women at the time. Colette died on Aug. 3, 1954, in Paris.

31

MARIE CURIE

(b. 1867–d. 1934)

Marie Curie was famous for her work on radioactivity and twice a winner of the Nobel Prize. With Henri Becquerel and her husband, Pierre Curie, she was awarded the 1903 Nobel Prize for Physics. She was the sole winner of the 1911 Nobel Prize for Chemistry. Marie Curie was the first woman to win a Nobel Prize, and she is the only woman to win the award in two different fields.

Maria Salomea Sklodowska was born on Nov. 7, 1867, in Warsaw, in what was then the Congress Kingdom of Poland, Russian Empire. From childhood she was remarkable for her prodigious memory, and at the age of 16 she won a gold medal on completion of her secondary education at the Russian lycée. Because her father, a teacher of mathematics and physics, lost his savings through bad investment, she had to take work as a teacher and at the same time took part clandestinely in the nationalist "free university," reading in Polish to women workers. At the age of 18 she took a post as a governess, where she suffered an unhappy love affair. However, from her earnings she was able to finance her sister Bronislawa's medical studies in Paris, France, with the understanding that Bronislawa would in turn later help her to get an education.

In 1891, Sklodowska went to Paris and—now using the name Marie—began to follow the lectures of Paul Appel, Gabriel Lippmann, and Edmond Bouty at the Sorbonne university. Sklodowska worked far into the night and completed degrees in physics and math. It was in the spring of 1891 that she met Pierre Curie.

Their marriage (July 25, 1895) marked the start of a partnership that was soon to achieve results of world significance, in particular the discovery of polonium (so called by Marie in honor of her native land) in the summer of 1898 and that of radium a few months later. Following Henri Becquerel's discovery (1896) of a new phenomenon (which she later called "radioactivity"), Marie Curie, looking for a subject for a thesis, decided to find out if the property discovered in uranium was to

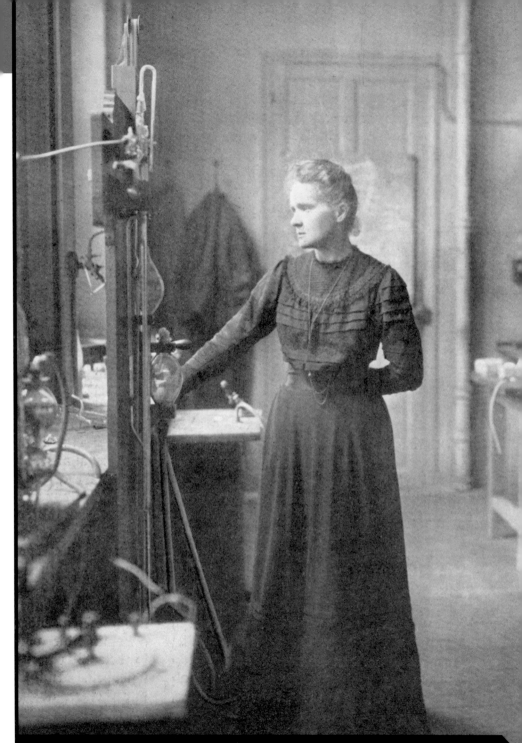

Colorized image of physicist and chemist Marie Curie, standing in her laboratory. Science Source/Photo Researchers/Getty Images

be found in other matter. She discovered that this was true for thorium at the same time as Gerhard Carl Schmidt did.

Turning her attention to minerals, she found her interest drawn to pitchblende, a mineral whose activity is superior to that of pure uranium. Pitchblende could be explained only by the presence in the ore of small quantities of an unknown substance of very high activity. Pierre Curie then joined Marie in the work that she had undertaken to resolve this problem and that led to the discovery of the new elements, polonium and radium.

While Pierre Curie devoted himself chiefly to the physical study of the new radiations, Marie Curie struggled to obtain pure radium in the metallic state—achieved with the help of the chemist André-Louis Debierne, one of Pierre Curie's pupils. On the results of this research, Marie Curie received her doctorate of science in June 1903 and—with Pierre—was awarded the Davy Medal of the Royal Society. Also in 1903 they shared with Becquerel the Nobel Prize for Physics for the discovery of radioactivity.

The birth of her two daughters, Irène and Ève, in 1897 and 1904 did not interrupt Marie's intensive scientific work. She was appointed lecturer in physics (1900) at the École Normale Supérieure for girls in Sèvres, France, and introduced there a method of teaching based on experimental demonstrations. In December 1904, she was appointed chief assistant in the laboratory directed by Pierre Curie.

The sudden death of Pierre Curie (April 19, 1906) was a bitter blow to Marie Curie, but it was also a decisive turning point in her career: henceforth, she was to devote all her energy to completing alone the scientific work that they had undertaken. On May 13, 1906, she was appointed to the professorship that had been left vacant on her husband's death; she was the first woman to teach in the Sorbonne. In 1908, she became titular professor, and in 1910, her fundamental treatise on radioactivity was published. In 1911, she was awarded the Nobel Prize for Chemistry, for the isolation of pure radium. In 1914, she saw the completion of the building of the laboratories of the Radium Institute (Institut du Radium) at the University of Paris.

Throughout World War I, Marie Curie, with the help of her daughter Irène, devoted herself to the development of the use of X-radiography.

In 1918, the Radium Institute, the staff of which Irène had joined, began to operate in earnest, and it was to become a universal center for nuclear physics and chemistry. Marie Curie, now at the highest point of her fame and, from 1922, a member of the Academy of Medicine, devoted her researches to the study of the chemistry of radioactive substances and the medical applications of these substances.

In 1921, accompanied by her two daughters, Marie Curie made a triumphant journey to the United States, where President Warren G. Harding presented her with a gram of radium that had been bought as the result of a collection among American women. Curie gave lectures, especially in Belgium, Brazil, Spain, and Czechoslovakia. She was made a member of the International Commission on Intellectual Co-operation by the Council of the League of Nations. In addition, she had the satisfaction of seeing the development of the Curie Foundation in Paris and in Poland the inauguration in 1932 in Warsaw of the Radium Institute, of which her sister Bronislawa became director.

On July 4, 1934, near Sallanches, France, Curie died as a result of leukemia caused by the action of radiation. In 1995, her ashes were enshrined in the Panthéon in Paris; she was the first woman to receive this honor for her own achievements. Her office and laboratory in the Curie Pavilion of the Radium Institute are preserved as the Curie Museum.

DIANA, PRINCESS OF WALES

(b. 1961–d. 1997)

The international obsession with Diana, princess of Wales, was a phenomenon of the age of television, tabloid journalism, phone taps, and telephoto lenses. For the 16 years from her wedding to her sudden death, millions followed the story of the young woman of ordinary abilities thrust into extraordinary circumstances, who rose above her problems to become one of the most admired women in the world.

Diana Frances Spencer was born on July 1, 1961, in Norfolk, England. Her parents, Edward John, Viscount Althorp (later the 8th Earl Spencer) and his first wife, Frances Roche, separated the summer Diana reached the age of 6. The divorce settlement gave the viscount custody of the children. Diana and her brother, Charles, spent the next few years shuttling back and forth between their parents' homes in the care of a series of nannies. Their older sisters, Sarah and Jane, were already away at boarding school. Diana tended her brother until she was old enough for boarding school. In September 1970, she went to Riddlesworth Hall, a preparatory boarding school in Norfolk. She was weak at academics but loved ballet, swimming, and tennis.

In 1974, Diana enrolled at West Heath School, a private secondary school near Sevenoaks, Kent. The West Heath curriculum emphasized community service. Diana enjoyed running errands for an older woman in the village and volunteering at a home for the mentally and physically handicapped.

She became Lady Diana Spencer in 1975, when her father inherited the Spencer earldom. The family moved from Park House to the huge estate of Althorp, 6 miles (9.7 kilometers) from Northampton. Diana left public school in 1977 and completed her formal education at age 16 with a few months at a finishing school in Switzerland.

Diana lived for a time with her mother in London. For her 18th birthday her parents gave her a London apartment, which she shared with friends. Soon after moving in she got regular part-time work as an assistant at a prestigious kindergarten.

Diana first met Charles Philip Arthur George, Prince of Wales and heir to the British throne, when he was courting her sister Sarah. Diana saw him more often after her sister Jane married Robert Fellowes, who worked in Buckingham Palace. Charles was nearly 13 years older than Diana. When he began courting Diana in the summer of 1980, public opinion declared her suitable. Reporters welcomed the announcement on Feb. 24, 1981, that the Prince of Wales would marry the 19-year-old kindergarten teacher. The wedding, on July 29, 1981, in St. Paul's Cathedral, London, was a spectacular royal occasion and a day of national festivity.

The couple made their home at Kensington Palace in London. Huge crowds turned out for their public appearances, virtually ignoring the prince in their eagerness to see the princess. Diana's flair for dress boosted the British fashion industry. Further excitement came with the announcement in November that the couple was expecting a child. Prince William Arthur Philip Louis was born on June 21, 1982. Prince Henry Charles Albert David followed on Sept. 15, 1984.

The fabled marriage quickly showed signs of strain; they were discovering they had few interests in common. Diana had little independence and courtiers fixed her schedule months in advance. She followed newspaper reports closely, her confidence bolstered by her popularity but shaken by any criticism. Behind a public pretense, her private life was marked by eating disorders, depression, and occasional threats of suicide.

In about 1986, however, Diana began to discover a fresh sense of purpose. She started to speak out for the sick, the destitute, children, and the elderly. She had always been compassionate and maternal and now she showed that, when motivated, she could also do her homework and speak intelligently in public. Her involvement in any cause or event attracted tremendous media interest. Although she often complained of being hounded by aggressive photographers known as paparazzi, she used the press to draw public attention and financial contributions to the causes she espoused.

The separation of Diana and Charles was announced in the House of Commons on Dec. 9, 1992. Diana threw herself into her work on behalf of a variety of causes: she comforted AIDS patients, the homeless, battered women, and sexually abused children; worked to prevent drug addiction and leprosy; and promoted the Red Cross and the needs of developing countries. In December, she announced her withdrawal from many public duties to give herself "time and space." Although the queen stopped sending her abroad to represent Britain, the princess continued to travel as a patron for selected private charities.

Media scrutiny reached its peak in 1994 and 1995, when both Prince Charles and Princess Diana revealed that they had engaged in extramarital affairs. The two ultimately divorced on Aug. 28, 1996. Diana kept the title Princess of Wales but was forced to relinquish the title Her Royal Highness.

In the months after her divorce, Diana led a crusade against the manufacture and use of antipersonnel land mines, which had maimed countless civilians in war-torn regions around the world. Her earnest devotion to human needs combined with her charismatic presence made the princess of Wales the most popular royal figure in Britain.

During the summer of 1997, the London tabloids reveled in Diana's romance with Emad Mohamed (Dodi) al-Fayed, an Egyptian-born multimillionaire whose father owned Harrods department store in London. Photographs of the pair sold for huge sums. On August 30, in Paris, France, a group of paparazzi pursued a car carrying Diana and Fayed. The car careened off the wall of an underground tunnel and into a support pillar. The driver and Fayed died immediately. A Welsh bodyguard was seriously injured but survived. Princess Diana was rushed to a nearby hospital and was pronounced dead in the early hours of Aug. 31, 1997. Britain went into national mourning. Diana's funeral in Westminster Abbey on Saturday, September 6, was televised around the world.

MARLENE DIETRICH

(b. 1901–d. 1992)

The German-born American film actress and entertainer developed an aura of sophistication and languid sensuality that made her one of the most glamorous of film stars.

She was born Marie Magdalene Dietrich on Dec. 27, 1901, in Berlin, Germany. Her father, Royal Prussian police officer Ludwig Dietrich, died when she was very young, and her mother remarried a cavalry officer, Edouard von Losch. Dietrich studied at a private school and learned both English and French by the age of 12. As a teenager she studied to be a concert violinist, but a wrist injury forced her to abandon her plans. She then turned to acting and changed her name to Marlene.

In 1929, director Josef von Sternberg saw Dietrich in a show in Germany and cast her as Lola-Lola, the sultry and world-weary female lead in *Der blaue Engel* (1930; *The Blue Angel*), Germany's first talking film. The film's success catapulted Dietrich to stardom. Von Sternberg took her to the United States and signed her with Paramount Pictures. She developed her femme fatale film persona with von Sternberg in *Morocco* (1930), *Dishonored* (1931), *Shanghai Express* (1932), *Blond Venus* (1932), *The Scarlet Empress* (1934), and *The Devil Is a Woman* (1935). The films became legendary for von Sternberg's elaborate visual style and obsessive exploration of his star's sexual ambiguity.

After breaking with von Sternberg, Dietrich revealed her talent as a comedienne in *Desire* (1936) and *Destry Rides Again* (1939). Dietrich's great popularity made her a trendsetter; her adoption of trousers (pants) and other masculine clothes helped launch an American fashion craze.

During World War II, Dietrich refused to work in Germany despite personal appeals made by Adolf Hitler, and her films were temporarily banned there. She became a United States citizen in 1937 and from 1943 to 1946 made more than 500 personal appearances before Allied troops. After the war she continued to make successful films, such as *A Foreign Affair* (1948), *The Monte Carlo Story* (1956), *Witness for the Prosecution* (1957), *Touch of Evil* (1958), and *Judgment at Nuremberg* (1961). She was also a popular nightclub performer. In 1978, after a period of retirement from the screen, she appeared in the film *Just a Gigolo*.

Dietrich's autobiography, *Ich bin, Gott sei Dank, Berlinerin* (*I Am, Thank God, a Berliner*; published in English as *Marlene*), appeared in 1987. She died in Paris on May 6, 1992.

DOROTHEA LYNDE DIX

(b. 1802–d. 1887)

A social reformer and humanitarian, Dorothea Lynde Dix devoted her life to the welfare of the mentally ill and the handicapped. Through her efforts, special hospitals for mental patients were built in more than fifteen states, and in Canada, Europe, and Japan.

Dix was born on April 4, 1802, in Hampden, Maine. She left her unhappy home at age 12 to live and study in Boston with her grandmother. By age 14 she was teaching in a school for young girls in Worcester, Massachusetts, employing a curriculum she created herself that stressed the natural sciences and the responsibilities of ethical living. In 1821, she opened a school for girls in Boston, where until the mid-1830s periods of intensive teaching were interrupted by periods of ill health. She eventually abandoned teaching and left Boston.

After nearly two years in England, Dix returned to Boston, still a semi-invalid, and that she had inherited a sum of money sufficient to support her comfortably for life. But her Calvinist beliefs kept her from being inactive. Thus in 1841, when a young clergyman asked her to begin a Sunday school class in the East Cambridge House of Correction in Massachusetts, she accepted the challenge.

While teaching at the prison, she first observed the inhumane treatment of insane and mentally disturbed persons, who were jailed with criminals. They were left unclothed, in darkness, without heat or sanitary facilities; some were chained to the walls and beaten with whips. Dix traveled for nearly two years throughout the state, observing similar conditions in each institution she examined. In January 1843, she submitted to the Massachusetts legislature a detailed report of her thoroughly documented findings. Her dignity, compassion, and determination were effective in helping to pass a bill for the enlargement of the Worcester Insane Asylum. Dix then moved on to Rhode Island and later New York.

Over the next 40 years, Dix inspired legislators in the United States and Canada to establish state hospitals for the mentally ill. Her efforts directly effected the building of thirty-two institutions in the United States. She carried on her work even while on a tour of Europe while recovering from illness in 1854–56. In Italy she prevailed upon Pope Pius IX to see for himself the atrocious conditions she had discovered.

Where new institutions were not required, she fostered the reorganization, enlargement, and restaffing—with well-trained, intelligent personnel—of already existing hospitals. In 1845, she published *Remarks on Prisons and Prison Discipline in the United States* to advocate reforms in the treatment of ordinary prisoners.

In 1861, Dix was appointed superintendent of army nurses for Civil War service. She was ill-suited to administration, however, and had great difficulty with the post. After the war she returned to her work with hospitals. Dix died on July 17, 1887, in Trenton, N.J., in a hospital that she had founded.

ISADORA DUNCAN
(b. 1877/78–d. 1927)

One of the first to raise the status of interpretive dance to that of creative art was Isadora Duncan. She helped free Western dance from its reliance on strict formulas and displays of mere technique, paving the way for the development of modern dance. She was controversial in both her professional and private lives.

She was born Angela Duncan in San Francisco, Calif. Her birth date is generally believed to be May 27, 1878, though her baptismal certificate records it as May 26, 1877. She rejected, even as a child, the rigidity of classical ballet and sought a more natural way of expressing herself through dance. She had changed her name to Isadora by 1894. Her first public appearances, in Chicago and New York City, were not successful, and she left at age 21 to seek recognition abroad. Her free-form style was enthusiastically welcomed in England and elsewhere in Europe. She opened dance schools in France, Germany, Russia, and the United States.

The first Western dancer to perform barefoot and without tights, Duncan preferred a filmy, loose-fitting tunic. Her simple, expressive movements were often based on poses from ancient Greek sculpture. Her dances consisted more of improvisational movements than of predetermined ones, and they were, therefore, seldom repeated. She danced to the music of the master composers, a choice that was at first criticized. Her considerable influence on modern dance occurred mostly after her death.

Duncan had two children out of wedlock, both of whom died in an accident in 1913. In 1922, she married a Russian poet 17 years younger than she. His increasing mental instability turned him against her, and he returned to the Soviet Union and committed suicide in 1925. Duncan lived the last years of her life in Nice, France. She died there on Sept. 14, 1927.

KATHERINE DUNHAM

(b. 1909–d. 2006)

A dancer, choreographer, anthropologist, and social activist, Katherine Dunham was instrumental in changing the status of the black dancer in America from entertainer to artist. Her dances incorporated elements from traditional Caribbean and African dance styles into ballet, modern dance, jazz, and theater.

Dunham was born in Chicago on June 22, 1909. She taught dance lessons to help pay for her education at the University of Chicago. As a graduate student in anthropology in the mid-1930s, she conducted dance research in the Caribbean. Back in the United States she formed an all-black dance troupe, which in 1940 performed her "Tropics and Le Jazz Hot," a revue that incorporated her Caribbean research as well as African American dance styles. Critics applauded her work, and in 1943, the company began the first of many successful tours of the United States, Canada, and later Europe. Among her major works were *L'Ag'Ya*, *Rites de Passage*, and *Choros*. She opened dance schools in New York City and Chicago, and many students of her technique went on to become prominent in the dance world.

Dunham choreographed also for the Broadway stage, the opera, and films. She was artistic and technical director for the president of Senegal in the late 1960s and later a professor at Southern Illinois University. She opened the Katherine Dunham Museum and Children's Workshop in East St. Louis, Ill. An autobiography of her early life, *A Touch of Innocence*, was published in 1959. Dunham died on May 21, 2006, in New York City.

AMELIA EARHART

(b. 1897–d. 1937)

O ne of the most intriguing mysteries of the 20th century involves what happened to celebrated American aviator Amelia Earhart as she attempted to fly around the world. Her disappearance was a sad end to the life story of the first American woman to fly solo across the Atlantic Ocean.

Earhart was born on July 24, 1897, in Atchison, Kan., but moved with her family to Chicago in 1916. During World War I, she worked as a military nurse in Canada, and for several years after the war she was a social worker in Boston. She learned to fly (against her family's wishes) in 1920–21 and in 1922 bought her first plane, a Kinner Canary.

Earhart first gained fame in 1928, when she was the first woman to fly across the Atlantic Ocean—even

Aviatrix Amelia Earhart, sitting in a plane's cockpit. © AP Images

though only as a passenger. Her reflections on that flight were published as *20 Hrs., 40 Min.* Four years later, in May 1932, she made a solo flight across the Atlantic, followed by several solo long-distance flights in the United States.

Earhart was greatly interested in the development of commercial aviation and took an active role in opening the field to women. For a time she served as an officer of the Luddington line, which operated one of the first regular passenger services between New York City and Washington, D.C. In January 1935, she made a solo flight from Hawaii to California.

In June 1937, she and her co-pilot, Lieutenant Commander Fred J. Noonan, left Miami, Florida, on an around-the-world flight attempt in a twin-engine Lockheed aircraft. On July 2, the plane vanished near

Howland Island in the South Pacific. The world waited with fascination as search teams from the United States Army and Navy, along with the Japanese navy, converged on the scene. But not she, Noonan, or the plane was ever found. As time went on, questions were raised about the flight. Was it simply an around-the-world adventure, or was she perhaps sent to spy on Japanese war preparations for the United States government? Historians have claimed that she was almost certainly forced down and killed by the Japanese.

After her disappearance, Earhart's husband, publisher George P. Putnam, wrote her biography, *Soaring Wings*. The book was published in 1939.

SHIRIN EBADI

(b. 1947–)

An Iranian lawyer, writer, and teacher, Shirin Ebadi received the Nobel Peace Prize in 2003 for her efforts to promote democracy and human rights, especially those of women and children in Iran. She was the first Muslim woman and the first Iranian to receive the award.

Shirin Ebadi was born on June 21, 1947, in Hamadan, Iran, but was raised in Tehran. She earned a law degree from the University of Tehran in 1969. That same year she began an apprenticeship at the Department of Justice and became one of the first women judges in Iran. She also earned a doctorate in private law from the University of Tehran in 1971. From 1975 to 1979, she was head of the city court of Tehran.

After militant Islamic revolutionaries took control of Iran in 1979, women's roles were limited. Ebadi and her female co-workers were forbidden to serve as judges and were instead given clerk duties. When they spoke out against their treatment, they were given higher roles within the Department of Justice but did not regain their previous positions. Ebadi resigned in protest. She then tried to practice law, but, under the same restrictive policies, she was denied a license. That changed in 1992, at which time she gained a license and began her own law practice. In this capacity Ebadi defended women and dissidents, representing many people who had come into opposition with the Iranian government. In

2000, she was found guilty of "disturbing public opinion" after she distributed evidence implicating government officials in the 1999 murders of students at the University of Tehran. She initially was given a prison term, barred from practicing law for five years, and fined, although her sentence was later suspended.

Ebadi wrote numerous books on the subject of human rights, including *The Rights of the Child: A Study of Legal Aspects of Children's Rights in Iran* (1994), *History and Documentation of Human Rights in Iran* (2000), and *The Rights of Women* (2002). She also was founder and head of the Association for Support of Children's Rights in Iran.

MARY BAKER EDDY

(b. 1821–d. 1910)

M ary Baker Eddy's family background and early life greatly influenced her interest in religious reform. In 1866, she founded the religious denomination known as Christian Science.

She was born Mary Baker on July 16, 1821, on a farm near Concord, N.H. As a child she had little formal education because of persistent ill health. As a teenager, she rebelled with others of her generation against what she called her father's "relentless theology." Although she believed in a benign God, she continued to ask how the reality of a God of love could possibly be reconciled with the existence of a world filled with so much misery and pain.

For many years her health was bad, and she turned to the Bible for consolation. In the early 1860s, she met and was healed by Phineas P. Quimby, who performed remarkable cures without medication. In 1866, following his death, she suffered a severe fall. On the third day after her injury, when she lay apparently near death, she called for her Bible and read the account in Matthew 9 of how Jesus healed the palsied man. She recovered in a seemingly miraculous manner. This experience led her to the discovery of the principle of Christian Science. There followed years of thought and study of the Bible, resulting in 1875 in her book *Science and Health with Key to the Scriptures*, the textbook of Christian Science.

45

Among the students who gathered around her was Asa Gilbert Eddy, whom she married in 1877. In 1879, Mary Baker Eddy organized the church in Boston, which came to be called the Mother Church, the First Church of Christ, Scientist. From this, branches spread to all parts of the United States and abroad. Eddy remained the active leader of the Christian Science movement until she died on Dec. 3, 1910.

ELEANOR OF AQUITAINE

(b. 1122–d. 1204)

In an age known largely for the exploits of kings, princes, dukes, and their warriors, Eleanor of Aquitaine stood out as one of the most remarkable of women. She was the wife and mother of kings and a dominant political force in the Europe of her time.

Eleanor was born in about 1122. Her father was William X, duke of Aquitaine. When he died in 1137, she inherited his domain, which was larger than that ruled by the king of France. The same year she married the heir to the French throne, who became King Louis VII a month afterward. During their 15-year marriage, she exerted considerable influence upon the running of the country and even accompanied him on the Second Crusade from 1147 to 1149. His jealousy led to separation, and the marriage was annulled, but she regained possession of Aquitaine.

In 1152, she married Henry Plantagenet, who became Henry II of England two years later. Together they had eight children, among whom were Richard I the Lion-Hearted and John, both of whom later became kings of England. This union brought together England, Aquitaine, Anjou, and Normandy under one rule. Two centuries later England's various French possessions became an underlying cause of the Hundred Years' War.

After the revolt of her sons against Henry II, Eleanor was kept in semi-confinement from 1174 to 1189, when Henry died. She then became active in affairs of state under her son Richard I and, after his death without an heir in 1199, under John. She worked for peace between France and England and helped preserve John's French domains. Eleanor died on April 1, 1204, in the monastery at Fontevrault in Anjou.

ELIZABETH I

(b. 1533–d. 1603)

Popularly known as the Virgin Queen and Good Queen Bess, Elizabeth Tudor was 25 years old when she became queen of England. The golden period of her reign is called the Elizabethan Age.

Elizabeth was born near London on Sept. 7, 1533. Her father was Henry VIII. Her mother was Anne Boleyn, the second of Henry's six wives. Henry's first wife, Catherine of Aragon, had only one surviving child, Mary. Henry wanted a male heir, so he asked the Pope to annul the marriage. Because the Pope refused, Henry broke away from the Roman Catholic Church and set himself up as head of the church in England. Then he married Anne. He was disappointed that Anne's child also was a girl. Before Elizabeth was three years old, he had her mother beheaded.

Henry gave Elizabeth a house of her own in the country. He paid little attention to her, and her governess complained that the princess "hath neither gown, nor kirtle, nor petticoat." Henry provided excellent tutors, however, and Elizabeth showed a love for learning. She received the type of education normally reserved for male heirs, with a course of studies centering on classical languages, history, rhetoric, and moral philosophy. One of her tutors, Roger Ascham, wrote: "Her perseverance is equal to that of a man, and her memory long keeps what it quickly picks up. She talks French and Italian as well as she does English. When she writes Greek and Latin, nothing is more beautiful than her handwriting. She delights as much in music as she is skillful in it."

Elizabeth became queen after the death of her half-sister, Mary, in 1558. At the beginning of her reign, England was in despair. The country had been weakened by war and religious strife, and the treasury was empty. Spain and France were powerful, and both wanted to rule England.

Elizabeth at once took the government into her own hands. She spent long hours with her secretaries, reading dispatches, dictating, and carefully examining the accounts. She had a genius for diplomacy, being both cautious and wily. She understood finance and was extremely frugal in the expenses of government. She hated war because it was wasteful of both men and money. The young queen chose as her chief minister Sir William Cecil (Lord Burghley), who was cautious and conservative like herself. For 40 years he was her mainstay in both home and foreign affairs.

During the first 30 years of Elizabeth's reign, England was at peace. Commerce revived, and English ships were boldly venturing overseas to the West Indies. There they came into conflict with Spain, which dominated the Caribbean region and claimed a monopoly of trade. English smugglers broke through the blockade and made huge profits by selling, in the West Indies, blacks they had seized in Africa. John Hawkins, Sir Francis Drake, and other English seamen also waylaid Spanish ships on their way home and seized their gold. Elizabeth aided the English privateers with ships and money and shared in their profits and stolen treasure.

King Philip II of Spain finally decided to put an end to these attacks by invading and conquering England. After years of preparation, Philip had assembled a great fleet of his best and largest warships, called by the Spanish the Armada. In 1588, the Armada sailed into the English Channel. The English were waiting for them with ships that were of newer design, smaller than the Spanish galleons but faster and more heavily armed. In a nine-day battle, the English inflicted terrible losses on the enemy.

Elizabeth's reign is most often defined in terms of the religious question, the defeat of the Spanish Armada, and a great flourishing of literature. Also important, however, were hundreds of laws on shipping, commerce, industry, currency reform, roads, relief for the poor, and agriculture. These laws shaped the policy of England for more than two centuries after Elizabeth's reign had ended. Elizabeth died on March 24, 1603, at the age of 69. She was buried with great magnificence in Westminster Abbey.

ELIZABETH II

(b. 1926–)

Like Elizabeth I of England's Golden Age, Elizabeth II came to the throne when she was 25 years old. "A fair and youthful figure," said Winston Churchill, "princess, wife, and mother, is heir to all our traditions and glories." The young queen had already won the affection of the British people by her charm and thoughtfulness, her modesty and simple dignity.

Named after three queens of England, Elizabeth Alexandra Mary was born on April 21, 1926, in London. Her father was Albert, duke of York, second son of George V. Her mother was Lady Elizabeth Bowes-Lyon, a member of the Scottish aristocracy. She was 4 years old when her sister, Margaret Rose, was born (Aug. 21, 1930). The princesses became close companions. Margaret Rose was lively and mischievous; Elizabeth, rather serious and thoughtful.

The princesses did not go to school but were taught by a governess, Miss Marion Crawford, a young Scottish woman. They rarely had the company of other children, but they had many pets, particularly horses and dogs. Occasionally their governess would give them a special treat by taking them for a ride in the Underground (subway) or on top of a bus.

Elizabeth's carefree days ended in 1936. George V, her grandfather, died early in that year, and before the year ended, her Uncle David (Edward VIII) had abdicated, meaning given up his claim to the throne. Elizabeth's father then became king, as George VI, and Elizabeth became heiress presumptive to the throne. The family moved into Buckingham Palace, the royal residence.

From this time, Elizabeth began to be trained for her future duties. From her parents and her grandmother, Queen Mary, she learned court etiquette and diplomatic practices. She studied the geography and history of the Commonwealth countries and the United States and was driven to Eton College for private lessons in constitutional law. She disliked arithmetic, and Queen Mary decided she would have little use for it.

Elizabeth was 13 when World War II broke out in 1939. The next year bombs began to fall on London, and the princesses were sent for safety to the grim fortress of Windsor Castle. On Oct. 13, 1940, Elizabeth returned to London to make her first broadcast, from a room in Buckingham Palace. In a clear confident voice, she told children everywhere that the children of Britain were "full of cheerfulness and courage." Before the war ended, she joined the women's branch of the Army and took training as an automobile driver and mechanic.

Elizabeth had the privilege, often denied to royalty, of marrying a man she loved. During the war she met Prince Philip, an officer in the Royal Navy. As a son of Prince Andrew of Greece, he was in line for the Greek throne, even though he had no Greek blood. Before King George announced the betrothal of the young couple, Philip dropped his title of prince to become a British citizen and took his mother's family name, Mountbatten. The king then made Philip duke of Edinburgh. On November 20, 1947, the couple was married at Westminster Abbey. A son, Prince Charles Philip Arthur George, was born on November 14, 1948, and a daughter, Princess Anne Elizabeth Alice Louise, on August 15, 1950. On February 19, 1960, the queen had a third child, Prince Andrew Albert Christian Edward. Her fourth child, Prince Edward Antony Richard Louis, was born on March 10, 1964. All these children had the surname "of Windsor," but in 1960 the queen announced that a new surname, Mountbatten-Windsor, would be borne by the third generation of her family.

Even before she became queen, Elizabeth served the government as a skilled ambassador. In 1948, she visited Paris and was acclaimed by the French people. In 1951, she and her husband made a six-week tour of all the provinces of Canada and then flew to Washington, D.C., for a brief visit with U.S. president Harry S. Truman and his wife.

The royal couple was in Kenya, on the first stage of a five-month tour to Australia and New Zealand, when George VI died on February 6, 1952. Elizabeth automatically became queen. On February 8, the queen took the oath of accession before the Privy Council. She was crowned at Westminster Abbey on June 2, 1953.

Elizabeth favored simplicity in court life and took an informed interest in government business. She traveled widely, throughout the United Kingdom and to many countries of the Commonwealth. Her reign was a time of unprecedented public scrutiny of the monarchy, especially after the failed marriage of her son Charles and Diana, princess of Wales, and Diana's death in 1997. Popular feeling in Britain turned against the royal family, which was thought to be out of touch with contemporary British life. In response, Elizabeth sought to present a less-stuffy and less-traditional image of the monarchy, which she did with some success. In 2002, she celebrated her Golden Jubilee, marking 50 years on the throne.

Ten years later, the queen celebrated her Diamond Jubilee, marking 60 years on the throne. The events included a parade of boats on the Thames River and a concert at Buckingham Palace. In cities throughout the United Kingdom and the Commonwealth, people lit a series of more than 4,000 beacons to commemorate the occasion. The queen also appeared at a church service at Saint Paul's Cathedral. Finally, a procession carried her back to Buckingham Palace, where she greeted the people of London from the balcony. The celebration of the Diamond Jubilee extended beyond the official events for the rest of the year.

ANNE FRANK

(b. 1929–d. 1945)

One of the most famous Jewish victims of the Holocaust, Anne Frank penned one of the world's most powerful accounts of Jewish life during World War II. Although Anne's diary did not pertain directly to the Holocaust, its readers became personally acquainted with one of the millions of Jewish victims of Nazi persecution, and the immense horror and tragedy of the Holocaust was transformed into a personal event.

Anne (Annelies) Marie Frank was born on June 12, 1929, in Frankfurt, Germany, to Otto and Edith Frank, both of whom came from respected German Jewish families. Anne and her older sister Margot grew up in a Germany that was becoming increasingly hostile to Jews, and the hostility worsened when the anti-Jewish National Socialist Party led by Adolf Hitler came to power in 1933. Realizing that the situation for Jews in Germany was becoming perilous, Otto Frank went to The Netherlands to set up a branch of his brother's company, the Dutch Opekta Company, in the city of Amsterdam. His family joined him soon after, and by the mid-1930s, the Franks had settled into a relatively happy existence free of persecution for their Jewish heritage. Anne quickly adapted to life in the new country and developed many friendships with Jewish and non-Jewish children alike.

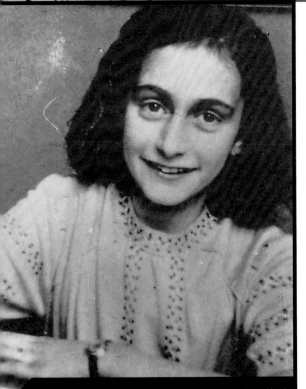

Undated photograph showing young schoolgirl Anne Frank. Anne Frank Center/AP Images

In 1939, the uneasy peace in Europe was shattered when German military forces began invading other European countries. World War II had commenced. In May 1940, The Netherlands surrendered to Germany and was quickly brought under the rule of German occupation. The Netherlands could no longer protect its Jewish population from Nazi persecution, and the occupying Nazi administration issued increasingly severe anti-Jewish decrees to isolate the Jews from the rest of the Dutch population. All Jews had to register their businesses and later surrender them to non-Jews. Otto Frank turned his business over to his non-Jewish colleagues, Victor Kugler and Johannes Kleiman. In 1941, Anne and Margot were no longer allowed to attend school with non-Jews. By 1942, all Jews aged 6 and older were required to wear a yellow Star of David on their clothes to mark them as Jews. Soon, Dutch Jews were being rounded up and deported to Westerbork prison camp in the northern Netherlands.

Meanwhile, Otto Frank was preparing the upper floors of the back annex attached to his office as a secret place where his family could hide from Nazi officials and sympathizers and escape deportation to the labor prison camps. He had solicited the help of Kugler and Kleiman as well as office workers Miep Gies, Jan Gies, and Bep Voskuijl to sustain them in hiding during the Nazi occupation. When Margot received a deportation notice on July 5, 1942, the family immediately went into hiding. The Franks were joined a week later by Otto's Jewish business partner Hermann van Pels, his wife Auguste, and their son Peter, and in November, by Fritz Pfeffer.

For more than two years, the people in the annex shared a confined space and lived under constant dread of detection by the Nazis. During the years in hiding, Anne developed from a girl into an adolescent. A diary she had been given on her 13th birthday, and took with her into hiding, became her best friend and confidante. She described the ups and downs of daily life in hiding and was candid about the others and unusually honest about the changes in herself. She wrote some of her diary notations into little stories, and rewrote a large portion from March to August 1944 after learning from a Dutch Free Radio broadcast that her diary could be of historical interest to others. The diary entries portrayed the adolescent Anne as a smart, free-spirited girl with a keen interest in boys and in cinema, who remained optimistic and dared to dream glamorous dreams despite her harrowing confinement.

On Aug. 4, 1944, a Nazi policeman and several Dutch collaborators raided the annex after receiving a tip from an informant. The residents of the secret annex were arrested and sent to Westerbork; a month later, they were on the last transport ever to leave Westerbork for Auschwitz concentration camp in Poland. Mrs. Frank died of starvation at Auschwitz. In October, Anne and Margot were transported from Auschwitz to Bergen-Belsen concentration camp in northwest Germany. There, the sisters soon contracted typhus. They died within weeks of each other in March 1945, a month before the camp was liberated by Allied troops. Otto Frank was the only resident of the annex to survive the Holocaust.

Anne's notebooks were found scattered on the floor of the empty hiding place by Miep Gies and Bep Voskuijl after the raid. Miep kept the diary in hopes of returning it to its owner, but she gave it to Otto when she learned that Anne had died. Following the suggestion of friends, Otto decided to publish Anne's diary, and in 1947, the diary—under the title *Het Achterhuis* (*The Secret Annex*, the title Anne had chosen herself)— was published in The Netherlands. Eventually, the diary was translated into more than 55 languages and became one of the most widely read books in the world. The popularity and emotional resonance of Anne

Frank's diary even led to dramatic renditions of the events recorded in the diary. A successful stage production of the Pulitzer Prize-winning play, *The Diary of Anne Frank*, premiered in 1955, and a film adaptation of the play was released in 1959.

In 1957, when the demolition of the secret annex was imminent, a number of prominent citizens of Amsterdam established the Anne Frank Foundation to preserve the annex on Prinsengracht 263. The house was transformed into a museum known as the Anne Frank House.

ROSALIND FRANKLIN

(b. 1920–d. 1958)

A British biophysicist, Rosalind Franklin is best known for her contributions to the discovery of the molecular structure of deoxyribonucleic acid (DNA), which is the chief substance composing chromosomes and genes, the hereditary material. When Francis Crick, James Watson, and Maurice Wilkins were awarded the 1962 Nobel Prize for Physiology or Medicine for determining the structure of the DNA molecule, many scientists believed that Franklin should have been honored with them.

Rosalind Elsie Franklin was born in London on July 25, 1920. She won a scholarship to Newnham College, Cambridge. After graduation in 1941, she began research on the physical structure of coals and carbonized coals. Working in Paris from 1947 to 1950, she gained skill in using X-ray diffraction as an analytical technique. (X-ray diffraction is a method of analyzing the crystal structure of materials by passing X-rays through them and observing the diffraction, or scattering, image of the rays.) Franklin used this technique to describe the structure of carbons with more precision than had previously been possible. She also determined that there are two distinct classes of carbons—those that form graphite when they are heated to high temperatures and those that do not.

In 1951, Franklin joined the King's College Medical Research Council biophysics unit. With Raymond Gosling, she conducted X-ray diffraction studies of the molecular structure of DNA. Based on these studies, she at first concluded that the structure was helical (having spiral arms).

Later research caused her to change her mind, and it was left to Watson and Crick to develop the double-helix model of the molecule that proved to be consistent with DNA's known properties. Some of the data used by those scientists in their successful effort, however, was first produced by Franklin.

In 1953, Franklin began work at the crystallography laboratory of Birkbeck College, London. There she published her earlier work on coals and helped determine the structure of the tobacco mosaic virus. She died on April 16, 1958, in London,

INDIRA GANDHI

(b. 1917–d. 1984)

An aggressive fighter in the struggle for Indian independence, Indira Gandhi was the first woman prime minister of India. She was the only child of Jawaharlal Nehru, who became India's first prime minister.

Indira Nehru was born on Nov. 19, 1917, in Allahabad, India. While she was growing up, her family was active in the nonviolent resistance movement led by Mahatma Gandhi against Great Britain's colonial rule of India. At the age of 12, she joined the movement by organizing thousands of Indian children to run errands and do odd jobs to aid the adults who were working for independence. She attended school intermittently in India and Switzerland, more often studying at home. In 1934, she studied art and dancing at the university at Santiniketa, and later attended Oxford University in England.

In March 1942, Indira Nehru married Feroze Gandhi, a friend from her student days in England. A few months later they were arrested after she spoke at a public meeting in defiance of a British ban. She was imprisoned for 13 months. After India achieved independence in 1947, Indira Gandhi toured refugee camps to aid victims of a Hindu-Muslim religious war. She accompanied her father on his official visits all over the world and campaigned for him during elections.

Beginning in 1959, Gandhi served for a year as president of the Indian National Congress, the majority political party. She became the minister of information and broadcasting in the cabinet of Prime Minister Lal

Indian Prime Minister Indira Gandhi in 1980.
Laurent Maous/Gamma-Rapho/Getty Images

Bahadur Shastri, who succeeded Nehru after his death in May 1964.

When Shastri died in January 1966, Gandhi was elected prime minister by the Congress Party. She was returned to office in the general elections of 1967 and 1971. Her government faced crop failures and food riots, poverty, student unrest, and resistance from the many different language groups to the adoption of Hindi as the nation's official language. In 1971, Gandhi led India in a successful war against Pakistan to separate East and West Pakistan and establish the nation of Bangladesh.

In 1975, Gandhi was convicted on two counts of corruption in the 1971 campaign. While appealing the decision, she declared a state of emergency, imprisoned her political opponents, and assumed emergency powers. Governing by decree, she imposed total press censorship and implemented a policy of large-scale sterilization as a form of birth control. When long-postponed national elections were held in 1977, Gandhi and her party were soundly defeated.

Reelected to Parliament in 1978, Gandhi was soon expelled and jailed briefly. While misconduct charges were still pending, she campaigned as an activist who would curb inflation and crime. A landslide victory returned her to office in 1980. Faced with the problem of Sikh extremists in the Punjab using violence to assert their demands in an autonomous state, Gandhi ordered the Indian army on June 6, 1984, to storm the Golden Temple at Amritsar, the Sikhs' holiest shrine, which had been converted into an armory. Hundreds of Sikhs died in the attack. Gandhi was assassinated by her own Sikh bodyguards as she walked to her office on Oct. 31, 1984.

ARTEMISIA GENTILESCHI

(b. 1593—d. 1652/53)

Artemisia Gentileschi was an Italian painter, daughter of Orazio Gentileschi, who was a major follower of the revolutionary Baroque painter Caravaggio. She was an important second-generation proponent of Caravaggio's dramatic realism.

Gentileschi was born on July 8, 1593, in Rome. She was a pupil of her father and of his friend the landscape painter Agostino Tassi. She painted at first in a style indistinguishable from her father's. Her first known work is *Susanna and the Elders* (1610), an accomplished work long attributed to her father. She also painted two versions of a scene already essayed by Caravaggio (but never attempted by her father), *Judith Beheading Holofernes* (*c.* 1612–13; *c.* 1620).

She was raped by Tassi, and when he did not fulfill his promise to marry her, Orazio Gentileschi in 1612 brought him to trial. During that event, she herself was forced to give evidence. Shortly after the trial she married a Florentine, and in 1616, she joined Florence's Academy of Design, the first woman to do so.

While in Florence she began to develop her own distinct style. Unlike many other women artists of the 17th century, she specialized in history painting rather than still life and portraiture. In Florence, she was associated with the Medici court, painting an *Allegory of Inclination* (*c.* 1616) for the series of frescoes honoring the life of Michelangelo in the Casa Buonarotti. Her colors are more brilliant than her father's, and she continued to employ the tenebrism—a style of painting that features interplay between shadow and light—made popular by Caravaggio long after her father had abandoned that style.

Gentileschi was in Rome for a time and in Venice. About 1630, she moved to Naples, and in 1638, she arrived in London, where she worked alongside her father for King Charles I. They collaborated on the ceiling paintings of the Great Hall in the Queen's House in Greenwich. After her father's death in 1639, she stayed on in London for at least several more years, painting many portraits and, according to her biographer, surpassing her father's fame.

Later, probably in 1640 or 1641, Gentileschi settled in Naples, where she painted several versions of the story of David and Bathsheba. Little is known of the final years of her life. She died in Naples in either 1652 or 1653.

NADINE GORDIMER

(b. 1923–)

South African novelist and short-story writer Nadine Gordimer often wrote on themes of exile and alienation. She received the Nobel Prize for literature in 1991.

Nadine Gordimer was born in Springs, Transvaal, South Africa, on Nov. 20, 1923, into a privileged, white, middle-class family. By the age of 9 she was writing, and she published her first story in a magazine when she was 15. Never an outstanding scholar, she attended the University of Witwatersrand for one year. Her wide reading, however, informed her about the world on the other side of apartheid—the official South African policy of racial segregation—and that discovery in time developed into strong political opposition to apartheid. She became a longtime member of the African National Congress, and because of her political views her books were banned in her country from 1958 to 1991. In addition to writing, she lectured and taught at various schools in the United States during the 1960s and 1970s.

Gordimer's fiction concerns the devastating effects of apartheid on the lives of South Africans. She examines how public events affect individual lives, how the dreams of one's youth are corrupted, and how innocence is lost. Her first book, a collection of short stories entitled *The Soft Voice of the Serpent*, appeared in 1952. The next year a novel, *The Lying Days*, was published. Both exhibit the clear, controlled, and unsentimental technique that became her hallmark. Her novel *The Conservationist* (1974) won the Booker Prize in 1974. Later works include *Burger's Daughter* (1979), the short-story collection *A Soldier's Embrace* (1980), *July's People* (1981), *A Sport of Nature* (1987), *My Son's Story* (1990), *None to Accompany Me* (1994), and *The House Gun* (1998).

MARTHA GRAHAM

(b. 1894–d. 1991)

Few individuals have contributed as much to the art of modern dance as the innovative choreographer and teacher Martha Graham. Her techniques were rooted in the muscular and nerve-muscle responses of the body to inner and outer stimuli. She created the most demanding body-training method in the field of modern dancing.

Martha Graham was born in Allegheny County, Pa., on May 11, 1894, and grew up there and in Santa Barbara, Calif. As a teenager she began studying dance at Denishawn, the dance company founded by Ruth St. Denis and Ted Shawn. Her debut was in *Xochitl*, a ballet based on an Aztec theme. It proved a great success both in vaudeville and in concert performances. Graham left Denishawn in 1923 to become a featured dancer in the Greenwich Village Follies. She also taught for a time at the Eastman School of Music in Rochester, N.Y. Her New York City debut as an independent artist was in 1926. Among the works on her program the next year was *Revolt*, probably the first dance of protest and social comment in the United States.

In a career spanning 70 years, Graham created 180 dance works. Some of these were based on Greek legends: *Night Journey*, first performed in 1947, about Jocasta, the mother of Oedipus; *Clytemnestra* (1958); and *Cave of the Heart* (1946), about the tragedy of Medea. *Letter to the World* (1940) was based on the life of poet Emily Dickinson. *Seraphic Dialogue* (1955) dealt with Joan of Arc, and *Embattled Garden* (1962) took up the Garden of Eden legend. Among her other works were *Appalachian Spring* (1944), with music by Aaron Copland; *Errand into the Maze* (1947); *Alcestis* (1960); *Acrobats of God* (1960); and *Maple Leaf Rag* (1990).

Graham announced her retirement in 1970. However, she continued to create new dances until her death in New York City on April 1, 1991.

HATSHEPSUT

(b. 1473 BCE–d. 1458 BCE)

Hatshepsut was one of only a few female kings of ancient Egypt, reigning from about 1473 to 1458 BCE. She attained unprecedented power for a woman, adopting the full titles and regalia of a pharaoh.

Hatshepsut, or Hatchepsut, was the elder daughter of the 18th-dynasty king Thutmose I and Queen Ahmose. Hatshepsut was married to her half-brother Thutmose II, who inherited his father's throne about 1492 BCE. She bore one daughter but no son. When Hatshepsut's husband died about 1479 BCE, the throne passed to his son Thutmose III, born to Isis, a lesser harem queen. Since Thutmose III was an infant, Hatshepsut acted as regent for the young king.

By the seventh year of Thutmose III's reign, Hatshepsut had herself crowned king, thus making the two co-rulers of Egypt (although Hatshepsut was the dominant king). Hatshepsut never explained why she took the throne or how she persuaded Egypt's elite to accept her new position. She may have been successful, however, because she had in place a group of loyal officials, many handpicked, who controlled all the key positions in her government.

Traditionally, Egyptian kings defended their land against the enemies who lurked at Egypt's borders. Hatshepsut's reign was essentially a peaceful one, and her foreign policy was based on trade rather than war. But scenes on the walls of her Dayr al-Bahri temple, in western Thebes, suggest that she participated in a short, successful military campaign in Nubia. Other scenes show a trading expedition in which gold, ebony, animal skins, baboons, processed myrrh, and living myrrh trees were brought back to Egypt. Hatshepsut also undertook an extensive building program, which included the temples of the god Amon-Re in Thebes and her Dayr al-Bahri temple.

Toward the end of her reign, Hatshepsut allowed Thutmose to play an increasingly prominent role in state affairs; following her death, Thutmose III ruled Egypt for almost 33 years. At the end of his reign, an attempt was made to remove all traces of Hatshepsut's rule. Her

A row of statues representing Hatshepsut as pharaoh, at her burial temple in Luxor, Egypt. EugenZ/Shutterstock.com

statues were torn down, her monuments were defaced, and her name was removed from the official king list. Early scholars interpreted this as an act of vengeance, but it seems that Thutmose was ensuring that the succession would run from Thutmose I through Thutmose II to Thutmose III without female interruption.

HILDEGARD

(b. 1098—d. 1179)

Hildegard of Bingen was a 12th century mystic, writer, and composer. She was also known as Sibyl of the Rhine for her gift of prophecy.

Hildegard was born in 1098, Böckelheim, West Franconia, Germany, of noble parents She was educated at the Benedictine cloister (convent) of Disibodenberg. Hildegard was 15 years old when she began wearing the Benedictine habit and pursuing a religious life. She became prioress (the nun in charge) of the cloister in 1136.

Hildegard had experienced visions since she was a child. It wasn't until she was 43 that she discussed those visions, and a committee of theologians confirmed their authenticity. A monk was appointed to help her record them in writing. The finished work, *Scivias* (1141–52), consists of 26 visions on such topics as the church, the relationship between God and man, and redemption. About 1147, Hildegard left Disibodenberg with several nuns to found a new convent at Rupertsberg, where she continued to exercise the gift of prophecy and to record her visions in writing.

A talented poet and composer, Hildegard collected 77 of her lyric poems, each with a musical setting composed by her, in *Symphonia armonie celestium revelationum*. Her numerous other writings include lives of saints; two works on medicine and natural history, reflecting a quality of scientific observation rare at that period; and extensive correspondence, in which are to be found further prophecies. For amusement, she also contrived her own language.

Hildegard traveled widely throughout Germany, evangelizing to large groups of people about her visions and religious insights. Though her earliest biographer proclaimed her a saint and miracles were reported during her life and at her tomb, she was never formally canonized. She is, however, listed as a saint in the Roman Martyrology and is honored on her feast day in certain German dioceses.

Hildegard died Sept. 17, 1179, in Rupertsberg, Germany. As one of the few prominent women in medieval church history, Hildegard became the subject of increasing interest in the latter half of the 20th century. Her writings were widely translated into English; several recordings of her music were made available; and works of fiction, including Barbara Lachman's *The Journal of Hildegard of Bingen* (1993) and Joan Ohanneson's *Scarlet Music: A Life of Hildegard of Bingen* (1997), were published.

DOROTHY CROWFOOT HODGKIN

(b. 1910–d. 1994)

English chemist Dorothy Hodgkin was awarded the Nobel Prize for chemistry in 1964 for her work in determining the structure of vitamin B12. In 1948, she and her colleagues made the first X-ray diffraction photograph of the vitamin. Until then normal chemical methods had revealed little of the structure of the central part of the molecule, at the heart of which is a cobalt atom. The atomic arrangement of the compound was eventually determined through the techniques that Hodgkin helped develop.

Dorothy Mary Crowfoot was born on May 12, 1910, in Cairo, Egypt. She studied in England at the Sir John Leman School and at Somerville College, Oxford. While at Oxford she studied X-rays of complicated macromolecules. In 1934, she and a colleague at Cambridge University made the first X-ray diffraction photograph of the protein pepsin. She returned to Somerville College later in 1934 as a tutor in chemistry. In 1937, she married Thomas Hodgkin, a lecturer and writer. From 1942 to 1949, she worked on a structural analysis of penicillin.

Hodgkin became a fellow of the Royal Society in 1947, professor of the Royal Society at Oxford University (1960–77), and a member of the Order of Merit in 1965. She spent the early 1960s in Africa at the University of Ghana, where her husband directed the Institute of African Studies. She was appointed chancellor of Bristol University in 1970 and an honorary fellow there in 1988. She was also a fellow of Wolfson College, Oxford (1977–83). Hodgkin died on July 29, 1994, in Shipston-on-Stour, Warwickshire, England.

KAREN HORNEY

(b. 1885–d. 1952)

German-born psychoanalyst Horney stressed social and environmental factors as determining individual personality traits and causing neuroses and personality disorders. In this she departed from the approach of Sigmund Freud, objecting to his concepts of libido, death instinct, and penis envy.

Horney was born Karen Danielsen in Hamburg, Germany, on Sept. 16, 1885. She received her medical degree from the University of Berlin in 1912 and trained in psychoanalysis with an associate of Freud named Karl Abraham. From 1915 to 1920, she did outpatient and clinical work at Berlin hospitals, and for the next 12 years she held a private practice and taught at the Berlin Psychoanalytic Institute.

After coming to the United States in 1932, she became associate director of the Chicago Institute for Psychoanalysis. She moved to New York City in 1934 to teach at the New School for Social Research and returned to private practice.

In her early books, *The Neurotic Personality of Our Time* (1937) and *New Ways in Psychoanalysis* (1939), Horney argued that Freud's idea of penis envy treated female psychology as an offshoot of male psychology. She also believed that the ways in which a child copes with anxiety eventually can give rise to persistent and irrational needs. Two of her later books are *Our Inner Conflicts* (1945) and *Neurosis and Human Growth* (1950).

Horney died in New York City on Dec. 4, 1952. The Karen Horney Foundation was established in New York the year of her death and gave rise in 1955 to the Karen Horney Clinic. Horney's analysis of the causes and the dynamics of neurosis and her revision of Freud's theory of personality have remained influential.

HYPATIA

(b. 355–d. 415)

Ancient Egyptian scholar Hypatia lived in Alexandria, Egypt, during the final years of the Roman Empire. She was the world's leading mathematician and astronomer of the time, and was also an important teacher of philosophy. She became a powerful symbol of female learning and science, as well as scholarly pursuits in the face of ignorant prejudice.

The year of Hypatia's birth is uncertain; she may have been born around 355. She was the daughter of Theon of Alexandria, a leading mathematician and astronomer who belonged to the Alexandrian Museum, a famous center of learning. Theon taught Hypatia mathematics, science, literature, philosophy, and art.

Hypatia continued her father's program. She wrote commentaries on works of geometry, number theory (an advanced branch of arithmetic), and astronomy. Unfortunately, none of her works has survived. Hypatia was also a popular teacher and lecturer on philosophy, attracting many loyal students and large audiences. She rose to become head of Alexandria's Neoplatonist school of philosophy, a school whose basic ideas derived from Plato.

Hypatia lived during a difficult time in Alexandria's history. The city was embroiled in a bitter religious conflict between Christians, Jews, and pagans (who believed in many gods). In 391, the Christian bishop of Alexandria had a pagan temple destroyed, even though it contained an important collection of classical literature that could not be replaced. Although Hypatia's teachings were not religious, some Christians saw them as pagan. Her views became less accepted in the city. In March 415, Hypatia was brutally murdered by a mob of Christian extremists.

IRENE

(b. 752—d. 803)

Irene was a Byzantine ruler and saint of the Greek Orthodox Church. She was instrumental in restoring the use of icons in the Eastern Roman Empire.

Irene was born in *c.* 752 in Athens. As the wife of the Byzantine emperor Leo IV, she became, on her husband's death in September 780, guardian of their 10-year-old son, Constantine VI, and co-emperor with him. Later in that year she crushed what seems to have been a plot by the Iconoclasts (opposers of the use of icons, or religious images) to put Leo's half-brother, Nicephorus, on the throne.

Irene favored the restoration of the use of icons, which had been prohibited in 730. She had Tarasius, one of her supporters, elected patriarch of Constantinople and then summoned a general church council on the subject. When it met in Constantinople in 786, the council was broken up by Iconoclast soldiers stationed in that city. Another council, which is recognized by both the Roman Catholic and Eastern Orthodox churches as the Seventh Ecumenical Council, met at Nicaea in 787 and restored the cult of images.

As Constantine approached maturity, he grew resentful of his mother's controlling influence in the empire. An attempt to seize power was crushed by the empress, who demanded that the military oath of fidelity should recognize her as senior ruler. Anger at the demand prompted the administrative divisions of Asia Minor to open resistance in 790. Constantine VI was proclaimed sole ruler and his mother banished from court. In January 792, however, Irene was allowed to return to court and even to resume her position as co-ruler. By skillful intrigues with the bishops and courtiers she organized a conspiracy against Constantine, who, in 797, was arrested and blinded at his mother's orders.

Irene then reigned alone as emperor (not empress) for five years. In 798, she opened diplomatic relations with the Western emperor Charlemagne, and in 802, a marriage between her and Charlemagne was reportedly contemplated. The scheme was apparently cut short before they could wed. In 802, a group of officials and generals deposed her and placed on the throne Nicephorus, the minister of finance. She was exiled, first to the island of Prinkipo (now Büyükada) and then to Lesbos.

Irene died on August 9, 803, on the island of Lesbos. Her zeal in restoring icons and her patronage of monasteries ensured her a place among the saints of the Greek Orthodox Church. Her feast day is August 9.

ISABELLA I

(b. 1451—d. 1504)

Isabella I was the queen of Castile (1474–1504) and of Aragon (1479–1504), ruling the two kingdoms jointly from 1479 with her husband, Ferdinand II of Aragon (Ferdinand V of Castile). Their rule affected the permanent union of Spain and the beginning of an overseas empire in the New World, led by Christopher Columbus under Isabella's sponsorship.

Isabella—born on April 22, 1451, in Madrigal de las Altas Torres, Castile—was the daughter of John II of Castile and his second wife, Isabella of Portugal. Her early years were spent quietly with her mother at Arévalo. The younger Isabella was brought to court when she was 13 in order to be under the eye of King Henry IV, her older half-brother. She was recognized as the king's heiress by the agreement known as the Accord of Toros de Guisando (Sept. 19, 1468).

Illuminated illustration showing the Castillian Queen Isabella (center), *from the book* Devocionario de la Reina Juana la Loca. Alinari Archives/Getty Images

As heiress of Castile, the question of Isabella's future marriage became a matter of increasing diplomatic activity at home and abroad. Portugal, Aragon, and France each put forward a marriage candidate. Henry seems to have wanted his half-sister to marry Afonso V, king of Portugal. However, without Henry's approval, she married Ferdinand of Aragon in October 1469 in the palace of Juan de Vivero, at Valladolid. It was believed that Isabella had shown disobedience to the crown in marrying Ferdinand without the royal consent. Henry rejected Isabella's claim to the throne.

Although Isabella and Henry were to some extent reconciled, the long-threatened war broke out at once when the king died in 1474. The first four years of Isabella's reign were thus occupied by a civil war, which ended in defeat for her Castilian opponents and for the Portuguese king.

Upon the death of John II of Aragon in the same year, the kingdoms of Castile and Aragon came together in the persons of their rulers, Isabella and Ferdinand, respectively. Spain emerged as a united country, but it was long before this personal union would lead to effective political unification. Each kingdom continued to be governed according to its own institutions.

Isabelle and Ferdinand were certainly united in their desire to take over the kingdom of Granada—the last Muslim stronghold in Spain. The conquest, which began in 1482, proved difficult and drawn out, and it strained the finances of Castile. Isabella took a close interest in the conduct of the war and seems to have been responsible for improved methods of supply and for the establishment of a military hospital. In 1491, she and Ferdinand set up a forward headquarters at Santa Fe, close to their ultimate objective, and there they stayed until Granada fell on January 2, 1492.

While she was at Santa Fe, Christopher Columbus visited Isabella to enlist support for the voyage that was to result in the European settlement of America. Although the story of her offering to pledge her jewels to help finance the expedition cannot be accepted, and Columbus secured only limited financial support from her, Isabella and her councilors must receive credit for making the decision to approve the momentous voyage. The terms on which the expedition was to set out to discover a new route to the Indies were drawn up on April 17, 1492. The New World that was explored as a result of that decision was, with papal confirmation, annexed to the crown of Castile, in accordance with existing practice in regard to such previous Atlantic discoveries as the Canary Islands.

The queen and her advisers hardly needed Columbus to remind them of the opportunity now offered for the spreading of Christianity. Yet the unexpected discoveries quickly brought fresh problems to Isabella, not the least of which was the relationship between the newly discovered "Indians" and the crown of Castile. The queen and her councilors were more ready to recognize the rights of the Indians than was Columbus; she ordered some of those he had brought back as slaves to be released.

It is difficult to disentangle Isabella's personal responsibility for the achievements of her reign from those of Ferdinand. But, undoubtedly, she played a large part in establishing the court as a centre of influence. A policy of reforming the Spanish churches had begun early in the 15th century, but the movement gathered momentum only under Isabella.

One of the achievements of Isabella's last decade was undoubtedly the success with which she and Ferdinand, acting on her initiative, extended their authority over the military orders of Alcántara, Calatrava, and Santiago, thus giving the crown control over their vast property and patronage. Throughout her long reign, Isabella also strove to strengthen royal authority at the expense of the Cortes (Spanish parliament) and the towns. She died on Nov. 26, 1504, Medina del Campo, Spain.

JIANG QING

(b. 1914–d. 1991)

Jiang Qing was the third wife of Chinese communist leader Mao Zedong, and subsequently one of the most influential woman in the People's Republic of China—at least until Mao's death in 1976. As a member of the Gang of Four, the most powerful members of the political group responsible for implementing Mao's harsh policies, Jiang was convicted in 1981 of "counter-revolutionary crimes" and imprisoned.

Jiang was born in March 1914 in Zhucheng, China. She was reared by her relatives, and became a member of a theatrical troupe in 1929. Her activity in a communist-front organization in 1933 led to her arrest and detainment. Upon her release she went to Shanghai, where she was arrested again in 1934. Upon her second release she left for Beijing, but she later returned to Shanghai, where she played minor roles for the left-wing Diantong Motion Pictures Company under her new stage name, Lan Ping.

When the Japanese attacked Shanghai in 1937, Jiang fled to the Chinese Nationalist wartime capital at Chongqing, where she worked for the government-controlled Central Movie Studio until she crossed the Nationalist lines. She went through Xi'an to join the communist forces in Yan'an and started to use the name Jiang Qing.

While a drama instructor at the Lu Xun Art Academy, she met Mao for the first time when he gave a talk at the school. They were married in 1939. The marriage was criticized by many party members, especially since the woman whom Mao divorced before marrying Jiang was then hospitalized in Moscow. Party leaders agreed to the marriage on condition that Jiang stay out of politics for the next 20 years.

After the establishment of the People's Republic of China in 1949, Jiang remained out of public view except to serve as Mao's hostess for foreign visitors or to sit on various cultural committees. In 1963, however, she became more politically active, sponsoring a movement in the Peking opera and in ballet aimed at infusing traditional Chinese art forms with working-class themes. Jiang's cultural reform movement gradually grew into a prolonged attack on many of the leading cultural and intellectual figures in China, culminating in the Cultural Revolution that by 1966 had begun to sweep the country.

Jiang reached the height of her power and influence in 1966, winning renown for her fiery speeches to mass gatherings and her involvement with the radical young Red Guard groups of the revolution. One of the few people whom Mao trusted, she became the first deputy head of the Cultural Revolution and acquired far-reaching powers over China's cultural life. She oversaw the total suppression of a wide variety of traditional cultural activities during the decade of the revolution. As the revolution's initial fervor waned in the late 1960s, however, so did Jiang's prominence. She reemerged in 1974 as a cultural leader and spokeswoman for Mao's new policy of "settling down."

Mao died on Sept. 9, 1976, and the radicals in the party lost their protector. A month later, wall posters appeared attacking Jiang and three other radicals as the Gang of Four, and the attacks grew progressively more hostile. Jiang and the other members of the Gang of Four were soon afterward arrested. She was expelled from the Communist Party in 1977.

In 1980–81, at her public trial as a member of the Gang of Four, Jiang was accused of fomenting the widespread civil unrest that had gripped China during the Cultural Revolution, but she refused to confess her guilt. Instead, she denounced the court and the country's leaders. She received a suspended death sentence, but in 1983, it was commuted to life imprisonment. Her death in prison on May 14, 1991, was officially reported as a suicide.

JOAN OF ARC

(b. 1412–d. 1431)

O ne of the most romantic figures in European war history was Joan of Arc, a peasant girl who saved the kingdom of France from English domination. She has also been called the Maid of Orléans and the Maid of France. When she was only 17 years old, Joan inspired a French army to break the English siege of the French city of Orléans and to win other important victories.

Joan was born the daughter of a wealthy tenant farmer in the village of Domrémy, in the Meuse River valley, probably in 1412. From her mother she learned how to spin, sew, and cook, and also to love and serve God. She spent much of her time praying in church.

For almost 100 years, France and much of Europe had been fighting in what became known as the Hundred Years' War. The English occupied much of northern France and the Duke of Burgundy was their ally. Because the impoverished French king, Charles VII, had not yet been crowned, he was still called the Dauphin. Reims, where the coronation ceremonies for French kings had been held for 1,000 years, was in enemy hands. The valley where Joan lived was constantly overrun by armies and guerrilla bands.

Joan was only about 13 when she first saw a heavenly vision. She later claimed that St. Michael had told her to be a good girl, to obey her mother, and to go to church often. For some time, however, she told no one of the visions. When St. Catherine and St. Margaret commanded her to journey to the Dauphin in order to inspire his armies to clear the way to Reims for the coronation, she told her parents and others. Her father refused to let her go, but her friends, who believed that she was truly inspired, secured boy's clothing and a horse for her. Several rode with her on the long trip to the Dauphin's court at Chinon.

The Dauphin and his councilors were not entirely convinced of her mission, however. Months of doubt and indecision followed while she was questioned. Slowly, though, an army was gathered. The Dauphin equipped Joan with armor, attendants, and horses. When the army at last moved toward Orleans, Joan was not its commander, but her presence inspired the soldiers with confidence. At Orleans, after Joan disapproved of the plans made for entering the besieged city, her own plan was adopted. From the city she led a series of attacks that so harassed and discouraged the English that they withdrew. In one of the skirmishes Joan was wounded.

On May 8, 1429, the victory was celebrated by the first festival of Orleans. The army entered Reims on July 16. The next day the Dauphin was crowned king with Joan nearby.

A decision was made to attack Paris, but the new monarch's hesitation and indecision prevented Joan's soldiers from concerted attack. Nevertheless, Compiègne and other nearby towns were taken. A French attack on a Paris was driven back and Joan was again wounded. Charles VII disbanded his army for the winter and retired southward. In the spring Joan returned to Compiègne, now besieged by forces of the Duke of Burgundy. On May 23, 1430, during an attack that led into the Burgundian lines, Joan was separated from her soldiers and captured.

As a prisoner at Beaurevoir, she attempted to escape, but was injured in the leap from a tower. Later she was sold to the English, who vowed that she would be executed. They took her to Rouen, where she was held in chains. Although the English wanted Joan's death, they desired her to be sentenced by an ecclesiastical, or religious, court. She was charged with heresy and witchcraft.

Joan was handed over to a court on January 3, 1431. Her "trial" began on February 21 and continued intermittently for months. Joan's appeal to be sent before the Pope for judgment was denied. On May 23, she was condemned to be burned unless she recanted. She had been held for many months in chains, threatened with torture, and harassed by thousands of questions. In spite of all this, she had maintained her shy innocence, often confounding her oppressors with simple, unaffected answers to tricky questions. St. Catherine and St. Margaret, she said, still counseled her.

Faced with death in the flames, she recanted, but many historians think she did not understand what was meant in the statement of recantation. As a result, her punishment was commuted from death to life imprisonment.

This leniency enraged the English, however, and it was not long before she was accused all over again. On May 30, 1431, when she was only 19 years old, Joan was turned over to civil authority and burned to death at the stake.

Charles VII had made no effort to save Joan. Some 25 years later he did aid her family to appeal the case to the Pope, and in 1456, a papal court annulled the judgment of 1431. On May 16, 1920, Joan of Arc was canonized a saint by the Roman Catholic Church.

ELLEN JOHNSON-SIRLEAF

(b. 1938–)

On January 16, 2006, Johnson-Sirleaf was sworn in as president of Liberia. In her inaugural speech she vowed to end civil strife and corruption, establish unity, and rebuild the country's devastated infrastructure. Johnson-Sirleaf's victory in her country's 2005 presidential election was the culmination of a long and often hazardous political career and made the "Iron Lady" Africa's first elected woman head of state.

Ellen Johnson was born in Monrovia, Liberia, on Oct. 29, 1938, of mixed Gola and German heritage. (Her father was the first indigenous Liberian to sit in the national legislature.) She was educated at the College of West Africa in Monrovia and at age 17 married James Sirleaf (they were later divorced). In 1961, Johnson-Sirleaf went to the United States to study economics and business administration. After obtaining a master's degree in public administration from Harvard University in 1971, she entered government service in Liberia.

Johnson-Sirleaf served as assistant minister of finance (1972–73) under Pres. William Tolbert and as finance minister (1980–85) in Samuel K. Doe's military dictatorship. She became known for her personal financial integrity and clashed with both heads of state. During Doe's regime she was imprisoned twice and narrowly avoided execution. In the 1985 national election, she campaigned for a seat in the Senate while openly criticizing the military government, which led to her arrest and a 10-year prison sentence. She was released after a short time and was allowed to leave the country. During 12 years of exile in Kenya and the United States, she became an influential economist for the World Bank, Citibank Corp., and other international financial institutions. From 1992 to 1997, she was the director of the Regional Bureau for Africa of the United Nations Development Programme.

Johnson-Sirleaf ran for president in the 1997 election, representing the Unity Party. She emphasized her financial experience, her non-involvement in the civil war, and the personal qualities of compassion, sacrifice, and wisdom that she had developed as a mother of four. She finished second to Charles Taylor and was forced back into exile when his government charged her with treason. By 1999, Liberia had again collapsed into civil war. Taylor was persuaded to go into exile in Nigeria in 2003, and Johnson-Sirleaf returned to Liberia to chair the Commission on Good Governance, which oversaw preparations for democratic elections. In the runoff presidential election on Nov. 8, 2005, she won 59.5 percent of the vote against retired association football (soccer) legend George Weah, who turned down a post in her administration but later issued a public statement of support.

With more than 15,000 UN peacekeepers in Liberia and unemployment running at 80 percent, the new president faced serious challenges. In her first 100 days in office, Johnson-Sirleaf visited Nigeria and the United States to seek debt amelioration and aid from the international community, established a Truth and Reconciliation Committee to probe corruption and heal ethnic tensions, fired the entire staff of the Ministry of Finance, and issued a program for the expansion of girls' education. By late 2010, Liberia's entire debt had been erased, and Johnson-Sirleaf had secured millions of dollars of foreign investment in the country.

Johnson-Sirleaf was one of three recipients, along with Leymah Gbowee and Tawakkul Karman, of the 2011 Nobel Peace Prize for their efforts to further women's rights. Later in 2011, Johnson-Sirleaf was re-elected as Liberia's president.

IRÈNE JOLIOT-CURIE

(b. 1897–d. 1956)

I rène Joliot-Curie was a French physicist and chemist who received the 1935 Nobel Prize for Chemistry jointly with her husband, Frédéric Joliot-Curie. She was the daughter of the Nobel Prize–winning scientists Pierre and Marie Curie.

She was born Irène Curie on September 12, 1897 in Paris. From 1912 to 1914, she prepared for her *baccalauréat* at the Collège Sévigné and in 1918 became her mother's assistant at the Institut du Radium of the University of Paris. In 1925, she presented her doctoral thesis on the alpha rays of polonium. In the same year she met Frédéric Joliot in her mother's laboratory; she was to find in him a mate who shared her interest in science, sports, humanism, and the arts. The two were married on October 9, 1926.

Joliet learned more about laboratory techniques under the guidance of his wife. Beginning in 1928, they signed their scientific work jointly. For the next 30 years they continued to add to the work of the elder Curies. Their first efforts were directed at the study of atomic nuclei. Together they synthesized new artificial radioactive material. For their work they were awarded the Nobel Prize for Chemistry in 1935. During the late 1930s, they did experiments that led to the development of nuclear fission. After World War II, they were both active in the development of nuclear reactors and later in various peace movements.

In 1936, Joliet-Curie served as undersecretary of scientific research in the French cabinet in 1936. She died on March 17, 1956, in Paris.

HELEN KELLER

(b. 1880–d. 1968)

"Once I knew only darkness and stillness.... My life was without past or future.... But a little word from the fingers of another fell into my hand that clutched at emptiness, and my heart leaped to the rapture of living." This is how Helen Keller described the beginning of her "new life," when despite blindness and deafness she learned to communicate with others.

Helen Adams Keller was born on June 27, 1880, in Tuscumbia, Ala. Nineteen months later she had a severe illness that left her blind and deaf. Her parents had hope for her. They had read Charles Dickens' report of the aid given to another blind and deaf girl, Laura Bridgman.

Helen Keller (right) *meets with actress Patty Duke in 1961. Duke portrayed Keller as a young girl in the Broadway play and feature film of the same name,* The Miracle Worker. Nina Leen/ Time & Life Pictures/Getty Images

When Keller was 6 years old, her parents took her to see Alexander Graham Bell, famed teacher of the deaf and inventor of the telephone. As a result of his advice, Keller became a student of Anne Mansfield Sullivan—who herself had been almost blind in early life, but her sight had been partially restored—beginning on March 3, 1887. Sullivan became Keller's teacher and constant companion.

Keller soon learned the finger-tip, or manual, alphabet as well as Braille. By placing her sensitive fingers on the lips and throat of her teachers, she felt their motions and learned to "hear" them speak. Three years after mastering the manual alphabet, she learned to speak herself.

At the age of 20 she was able to enter Radcliffe College. She received her bachelor of arts degree in 1904 with honors. She used textbooks in Braille, and Sullivan attended classes with her, spelling the lectures into her hand.

Keller helped to found the Massachusetts Commission for the Blind and served on the commission. She raised more money for the American Foundation for the Blind than any other person. She lectured widely and received honors and awards from foreign governments and international bodies.

Keller's writing reveals her interest in the beauty of things taken for granted by those who can see and hear. Her books include *The Story of My Life* (1903); *Optimism* (also 1903), *The World I Live In* (1908), *Out of* the Dark (1913), *Midstream: My Later Life* (1929); *Journal* (1938), and *Let Us Have Faith* (1940).

At her home near Easton, Conn., Keller wrote and worked for the blind and deaf. She died at her home on June 1, 1968.

BILLIE JEAN KING

(b. 1943–)

Just three short years after turning professional in 1968, Billie Jean King became the first professional female athlete to be paid more than $100,000 in a single season (1971). Perhaps the greatest women's doubles player in tennis history, she was also an activist for women's rights. She helped to organize the Women's Tennis Association and to establish a women's pro tour in the early 1970s.

Billie Jean Moffitt was born in Long Beach, Calif., on Nov. 22, 1943. She began playing tennis at an early age. In 1965, she married Larry King (not the former CNN talk-show host), and in the 1970s the couple pioneered team tennis.

Billie Jean King holds the record for British titles with a total of 20 championships. She won the women's doubles at Wimbledon in 1961–62 and 1965 before achieving her first major singles triumph there in 1966. She also won the Wimbledon singles in 1967–68, 1972–73, and 1975; women's doubles in 1967–68, 1970–73, and 1979; and mixed doubles in 1967, 1971, and 1973–74.

King won the U.S. women's singles title in 1967, 1971–72, and 1974; women's doubles in 1964, 1967, 1974, 1978, and 1980; and mixed doubles in 1967, 1971, 1973, and 1976. She was the only woman to win U.S. singles titles on four surfaces—grass, indoor, clay, and hard court. With her victories in 1967, she was the first woman since 1938 to sweep the U.S. and British singles, doubles, and mixed doubles titles in a single season.

In a match billed as the Battle of the Sexes at the Houston Astrodome on Sept. 20, 1973, King defeated Bobby Riggs, a former Wimbledon and U.S. Open champion who had criticized the quality of women's tennis. The match set two records: The audience of

Tennis great Billie Jean King, holding aloft her second Wimbeldon singles trophy for pho-tographers at the All England Club, 1968. Central Press/Hulton Archive/Getty Images

more than 30,000 was the largest to witness a tennis event, and the $100,000 purse was the largest won by a player.

King retired from competitive tennis in 1984. In the mid-1990s, she served as coach for several Olympic and Federation Cup teams. King published two autobiographies, as well as other books on tennis. In 2009, she was awarded the U.S. Presidential Medal of Freedom.

CHRISTINE LAGARDE

(b. 1956–)

A French lawyer and politician, Christine Legarde was the first woman to serve as France's finance minister (2007–11). Legarde also has served as managing director of the International Monetary Fund, starting in 2011.

Christine Lagarde was born on January 1, 1956, in Paris and educated in the United States and France. After graduating (1974) from the prestigious Holton-Arms girls' college-preparatory school in Bethesda, Maryland, she studied at the Law School of the University of Paris X-Nanterre, where she lectured after graduation before going on to specialize in labor law, in which she obtained a postgraduate diploma. She also acquired a master's degree in English. In 1981, Lagarde joined the international law firm Baker & McKenzie in Paris. She was made a partner in 1987 and became the first female member (1995–99) of the executive committee. She was made chairman of the executive committee in 1999 (reelected 2002) and moved to Chicago. At Baker & McKenzie, she advocated a "client first" approach, whereby lawyers anticipated client needs rather than solely reacting to difficult situations. As a result, profits at the firm rose strongly.

While a member of the Center for Strategic & International Studies (CSIS), Lagarde led the U.S.-Poland Defense Industry Working Group, advancing the interests of aircraft companies Boeing and Lockheed Martin against those of Airbus and Dassault Aviation. In 2003, she was a member of the CSIS commission that culminated in a $3.5 billion contract for the sale of 48 Lockheed Martin jet fighters to Poland. Despite what struck some French observers as a conflict of interest, Lagarde in March 2004 received an appointment to France's highest order, the Legion of Honour, from Pres. Jacques Chirac, who described her as a role model and a charismatic leader.

Lagarde returned to France in June 2005 to join Prime Minister Dominique de Villepin's government as trade minister before becoming (briefly) minister for agriculture and fisheries in 2007. As trade minister she encouraged foreign investment in France and the opening of new markets for French products, particularly in the technology sector, helping exporters through the Cap Export mechanism, which she launched in September 2005.

In June 2007, Lagarde was designated finance minister by newly elected Pres. Nicolas Sarkozy. She was the first woman in the Group of Eight countries to hold this influential position. Her appointment reflected the end of a political leadership dominated by anti-globalization and the burgeoning (if tacit) acceptance of the unpleasant measures needed to revitalize France's increasingly uncompetitive and flagging economy. In contrast to her predecessors, Lagarde held the controversial view that the country's 35-hour workweek was a symbol of indolence. She advocated a stronger work ethic, a sentiment mirrored by the French business community. In June 2011, Lagarde was appointed managing director and chairman of the board of the IMF. The following month she officially replaced Dominique Strauss-Kahn, who had resigned in May of that year.

ROSA LUXEMBURG

(b. 1871–d. 1919)

Rosa Luxemburg was one of the foremost theoreticians of the Socialist and Communist movements in the early 20th century. Like Vladimir Lenin, she believed in the violent overthrow of the capitalist system. Unlike him, however, she was opposed to nationalism and emphasized internationalism, stressing revolutionary mass action that she believed would lead to more democratic organizations.

Rosa Luxemburg was born in Zamość, Russian Poland (now Poland), on March 5, 1871. The youngest of five children of a lower middle-class

Jewish family, she became involved in underground activities while still in high school. Like many of her radical contemporaries from the Russian Empire who were faced with prison, she emigrated to Zürich (1889), where she studied law and political economy, receiving a doctorate in 1898. While in Zurich, she became a founder of the Polish Social Democratic party, later to become the Polish Communist party.

In 1898, she married Gustav Lübeck, a German national. They settled in Berlin, a center of Socialist activity, where she gradually formulated her own distinct views and became involved in conflicts that divided the party.

Photo of theoretician revolutionary Rosa Luxemburg. Henry Guttmann/Hulton Archive/ Getty Images

The Russian Revolution of 1905 proved to be the central experience in Luxemburg's life. Until then, she had believed that Germany was the country in which world revolution was most likely to originate. She now believed it would catch fire in Russia. She went to Warsaw, participated in the struggle, and was imprisoned. From these experiences emerged her theory of revolutionary mass action, which she propounded in *Massenstreik, Partei und Gewerkschaften* (1906; *The Mass Strike, the Political Party, and the Trade Unions*). Luxemburg advocated the mass strike as the single most important tool of the working class, Western as well as Russian, in attaining a socialist victory.

Released from her Warsaw prison, she taught at the Social Democratic Party school in Berlin (1907–14), where she wrote *Die*

Akkumulation des Kapitals (1913; *The Accumulation of Capital*). At this time she also broke completely with the established Social Democratic party leadership.

Luxemburg opposed World War I because it undermined Socialist internationalism. She and her associate Karl Liebknecht formed the Spartacus League, dedicated to ending the war through a workers' revolution. In 1918, they founded the German Communist party.

Luxemburg remained a believer in democracy as opposed to Lenin's democratic centralism. She was never able, however, to exercise a decisive influence on the new party, for she and Liebknecht were assassinated in Berlin on Jan. 15, 1919, by reactionary troops.

WANGARI MAATHAI

(b. 1940–d. 2011)

Wangari Maathai was a Kenyan politician and environmental activist who was awarded the Nobel Peace Prize in 2004 for her "holistic approach to sustainable development that embraces democracy, human rights, and women's rights in particular." She became the first black African woman to achieve such an honor.

Wangari Muta Maathai was born on April 1, 1940, in Nyeri, Kenya. She attended college in the United States, receiving a bachelor's degree in biology from Mount St. Scholastica College (now Benedictine College) in 1964 and a master's degree from the University of Pittsburgh in 1966. In 1971, she completed her Ph.D. at the University of Nairobi, having the distinction of becoming the first woman in either East or Central Africa to earn a doctorate. After graduating, she began teaching in the Department of Veterinary Anatomy at the University of Nairobi, and in 1977 she became chair of the department.

Maathai was working with the National Council of Women of Kenya when she began to explore the idea that village women could improve the environment by planting trees. Her goal was twofold: to provide a fuel source for families and to slow the processes of deforestation and desertification. In 1977, she founded the Green Belt Movement to further her purpose, and by the early 21st century the organization had planted some 30 million trees. Organization members went on to start the Pan African Green Belt Network in 1986, which was dedicated to providing information about conservation and environmental improvement to world leaders. As a result of the organization's activism, similar movements were started in Tanzania, Ethiopia, Zimbabwe, and other African countries.

Wangari Maathai, presenting at the 2005 Live 8 Edinburgh concert, designed to raise awareness of world poverty and coinciding with the G8 economic summit that year in Scotland. MJ Kim/ Getty Images

Maathai's other interests included human rights, AIDS prevention, and women's issues. She often addressed these concerns at meetings of the United Nations General Assembly. In 2002, Maathai was elected to Kenya's National Assembly, and the next year she was appointed assistant minister of environment, natural resources, and wildlife. She was the author of several books, including *The Green Belt Movement: Sharing the Approach and the Experience* (1988), which detailed the history of the organization, and an autobiography, *Unbowed* (2007). In *The Challenge for Africa* (2009) she criticized Africa's ineffective leadership and prompted Africans to solve their problems without Western help. Maathai also contributed to such international periodicals as the *Los Angeles Times* and the *Guardian*. Maathai died on Sept. 25, 2011, in Nairobi, Kenya.

MARGARET I

(b. 1353–d. 1412)

M argaret I was regent of Denmark (from 1375), of Norway (from 1380), and of Sweden (from 1389). By diplomacy and war, she pursued dynastic policies that led to the Kalmar Union (1397), which united Denmark, Norway, and Sweden until 1523 and Denmark and Norway until 1814.

Born in 1353 as the daughter of King Valdemar IV of Denmark, Margaret was only six years old when she was betrothed to Haakon, king of Norway and son of King Magnus Eriksson of Sweden and Norway. The betrothal, intended to counter the dynastic claims to the Scandinavian thrones by the dukes of Mecklenburg and the intrigues of certain aristocratic factions within the Scandinavian countries, was endangered by the renewal in 1360 of the old struggle between Valdemar of Denmark and Magnus of Sweden. But military reverses and the opposition of his own nobility forced Magnus to suspend attacks in 1363. The wedding of Margaret and Haakon took place in Copenhagen in the same year.

Haakon's aspirations to become king of Sweden were destroyed when he and his father were defeated soon afterward by Albert of Mecklenburg, who bore the Swedish crown from 1364 to 1389. Haakon, however, succeeded in keeping his Norwegian kingdom, and it was there that Margaret spent her youth, under the tutelage of Märta Ulfsdotter, a daughter of the Swedish saint, Bridget. Margaret early displayed her talent as a ruler: she soon overshadowed her husband and appears to have exercised the real power. The couple's only child, Olaf, was born in 1370.

After her father's death in 1375, Margaret—over the objections of the Mecklenburgian claimants—was successful in getting Olaf elected to the Danish throne. Following Haakon's death in 1380, Margaret also ruled Norway in her son's name. Thus began the Danish-Norwegian union that lasted until 1814. Margaret secured and extended her sovereignty: in 1385, she won back the economically important strongholds on the west coast of Scandia from the Hanseatic League, and for a time she was also able to safeguard Denmark's southern borders by agreement with the counts of Holstein.

Margaret and Olaf, who came of age in 1385, were on the point of declaring war on Albert to enforce their claims to the Swedish throne when Olaf died unexpectedly in 1387. Deploying all her diplomatic skill, Margaret consolidated her position, becoming regent of both Norway and Denmark and, in the absence of an heir, adopting her six-year-old nephew, Erik of Pomerania. She then joined forces with the Swedish nobles, who had risen against the unpopular king Albert in a dispute over the will disposing of the lands of Bo Jonsson Grip, the powerful chancellor. By the Treaty of Dalaborg of 1388, the nobles proclaimed Margaret Sweden's "sovereign lady and rightful ruler" and granted her the main portion of Bo Jonsson Grip's vast domains. Defeating Albert in 1389, Margaret took him captive and released him only after the conclusion of peace six years later. His supporters, who had allied themselves with pirate bands in the Baltic Sea, did not surrender Stockholm until 1398.

Margaret was now the undisputed ruler of the three Scandinavian states. Her heir, Erik of Pomerania, was declared hereditary king of Norway in 1389 and was elected king of Denmark and Sweden (which also included Finland) in 1396. His coronation took place the following year in the southern Swedish town of Kalmar, in the presence of the leading figures of all the Scandinavian countries. At Kalmar the nobility manifested its opposition to Margaret's increasing exercise of absolute power. The two existing documents disclose traces of the struggle between two political principles: the principle of absolute hereditary monarchy, as expressed in the so-called coronation act, and the constitutional elective kingship preferred by some nobles, as expressed in the so-called union act. The Kalmar assembly was a victory for Margaret and absolutism; the union act—perhaps the medieval Scandinavian document most debated by historians—denoted a plan that failed.

Despite Erik's coronation, Margaret remained Scandinavia's actual ruler until her death. Her aim was to further develop a strong royal central power and to foster the growth of a united Scandinavian state with its center of gravity located in Denmark, her old hereditary dominion. She succeeded in eliminating the opposition of the nobility, in curbing the powers of the council of state, and in consolidating the administration through a network of royal sheriffs. In order to secure her position economically, she levied heavy taxes and confiscated church estates and lands exempt from dues to the crown. That such a policy succeeded without fatal strife to the union testifies to her strong political position as well as to her diplomatic skills and her ruthlessness. By adroitly using her relations to the Holy See, she was able to strengthen her influence over the church and on the politically important Episcopal elections.

Margaret's political insight was also evident in foreign affairs. Her main goals were to put an end to German expansion to the north and to extend and secure Denmark's southern borders, goals she tried to achieve through diplomatic means. An armed conflict did, however, break out with Holstein, and during the war Margaret died unexpectedly in 1412.

One of Scandinavia's most eminent monarchs, Margaret was able not only to establish peace in her realms but also to maintain her authority against the aspirations of German princes and against the superior economic power of the Hanseatic League. The united kingdom that she created and left as a legacy, whose cementing factor was a strong monarchy, remained in existence until 1523, albeit not without interruptions.

MARIA THERESA
(b. 1717–d. 1780)

C alled "the most human of the Hapsburgs," Maria Theresa was a key figure in the complex politics of Europe in the 1700s. Her father, the Holy Roman emperor Charles VI, tried to ensure her succession to his domains. She devoted much of her life to the fight to keep her lands.

Maria Theresa was born in Vienna on May 13, 1717. At the age of 23 she became archduchess of Austria and queen of Bohemia and Hungary. She also inherited outlying possessions of the house of Austria in Italy and the Netherlands. Various powers hoped to add to their territories at the expense of the inexperienced queen. Most determined of all her enemies was young Frederick II, King of Prussia.

Maria Theresa's father, Emperor Charles VI, was the last of the direct male line of the Austrian Hapsburgs. He had no sons, and the Hapsburg law forbade women to inherit Hapsburg lands. In order to secure his oldest daughter's succession, he drew up a revision of the law called the Pragmatic Sanction. After long negotiations he persuaded all the major powers of Europe—including Prussia—to agree to this international treaty. Before coming to the throne, Maria Theresa married Duke Francis of Lorraine.

Maria Theresa had been on the throne only two months when Frederick marched his army southward into Silesia, the fertile valley of the Oder River that stretched southeastward from his own Brandenburg. Her Hungarian subjects failed in their attempts to expel Frederick from Silesia.

Frederick's success encouraged other countries to ignore the Pragmatic Sanction. Most of the powers of Europe joined in the War of the Austrian Succession (1740–48). Maria Theresa found an ally in George II of Great Britain. As elector of Hanover, a German state, he feared the spread of Prussia's power. On the other side the chief allies were Prussia, France, Spain, and Bavaria. In America and on the high seas, the conflict raged between France and Great Britain as King George's War.

The treaty that ended the war was signed at Aix-la-Chapelle in 1748. It confirmed the loss of Silesia to Prussia but restored everything else to the situation at the opening of the war. Maria Theresa won recognition of the principle of the Pragmatic Sanction, and in 1745, the powers approved the election of her husband as Holy Roman emperor with the title of Francis I.

Maria Theresa's pride and her devout Roman Catholicism made her determined to recover her lost province from Protestant Prussia. She formed an alliance with Russia and then set about to win France as an ally against Prussia. To continue this complicated exchange of allegiances, Frederick then entered into an alliance with Great Britain.

Maria Theresa's foreign minister, Count Wenzel von Kaunitz, concluded the French alliance in 1756. This disturbed all existing international pacts. The "third Silesian war" began the same year and merged into a war between Britain and France for empire in America and in India. Frederick, though he had enemies on all sides, eventually prevailed. Russia concluded a peace with him, and he then turned upon the Austrians and drove them out of Silesia.

In 1772, Maria Theresa made up for the loss of Silesia by joining with Russia and Prussia in the first partition of Poland. Galicia was Austria's share. In 1779, she averted another war with Prussia by arranging the Peace of Teschen, the last significant act of her reign.

Maria Theresa had 16 children. To strengthen the alliance with France, she married her youngest daughter, Marie Antoinette, to the heir to the French throne. Her oldest son, Joseph II, assisted her in the government after the death of her husband. She carried out many reforms to strengthen the unity of her lands. She ruled as an absolute monarch, but she was one of the enlightened despots of the 18th century. She died in Vienna on Nov. 28, 1780. Joseph II succeeded her.

MARIE-ANTOINETTE

(b. 1755–d. 1793)

Frivolous and extravagant, Marie Antoinette, the queen of France and wife of Louis XVI, became the symbol of the people's hatred for the old regime during the French Revolution. According to legend, when informed that the poor people had no bread to eat, she responded, "Let them eat cake." Her extravagance contributed only slightly to France's staggering debt, but her callous disregard for the country's plight and her foreign connections made her the focus of hatred and distrust.

Marie Antoinette was born in Vienna on Nov. 2, 1755. She was the daughter of Emperor Francis I and Maria Theresa of Austria. France and Austria, long bitter enemies, made a treaty of alliance. To strengthen the alliance, Marie Antoinette was married to the Dauphin (heir to the French throne) in 1770. At that time she was 15 years old and the Dauphin 16.

The Dauphin was a well-meaning person, but he was dull and unsociable. His beautiful and vivacious young wife went her own way, bent on pleasure, and shocked the French court by disregarding its strict etiquette. In 1774 Louis XV died, and the Dauphin became king as Louis XVI. The country was almost bankrupt, but extravagance continued to be the rule at the Palace of Versailles. The people blamed much of their distress on the queen. On Oct. 5, 1789, after the French Revolution had begun, several thousand men and women walked from Paris to Versailles to present their demands to the king. They forced the royal family to return with them to Paris.

Bust of Marie-Antoinette, gracing the fireplace mantle of the queen's chamber in the French Palace of Versaille. DEA/G. Dagli Orti/De Agostini/ Getty Images

After months of being virtual prisoners in their palace in Paris, Marie Antoinette finally persuaded the king that they should flee the country. On the night of June 20, 1791, dressed as ordinary travelers, the family left by coach for the eastern border. Before they reached it they were recognized and forced to turn back. This incident strengthened the popular suspicion that the king and queen were plotting to bring about foreign intervention.

On Aug. 10, 1792, revolutionaries stormed the Palace of the Tuileries and massacred the Swiss Guards. The royal family was imprisoned. On September 22, France was proclaimed a republic. Louis XVI was beheaded on Jan. 21, 1793. On October 14, during the Reign of Terror, the queen was tried and condemned for treason. Two days later, she was put to death on the guillotine.

MARY I

(b. 1516–d. 1558)

Mary I has come down in history with the unpleasant name of Bloody Mary because of the religious persecutions of her reign. A devout Catholic, she targeted Protestants in a vain attempt to win England back to the Roman Catholic Church.

Mary was born on February 18, 1516, at Greenwich Palace, near London. Also called Mary Tudor, she was the daughter of King Henry VIII and his first wife, Catherine of Aragon. She was the Queen of England from 1553 to 1558. None of Catherine's other children lived, and the king worried that he did not have a son to succeed him. Henry decided to divorce Catherine in order to marry Anne Boleyn, but the Pope refused to grant the divorce. Henry then abandoned Catholicism and created the Protestant Church of England. As head of this new church, Henry granted himself the divorce and married Anne.

Henry's new marriage radically disrupted Mary's life. Mary was declared an illegitimate child, meaning that she would not inherit the throne. When Anne Boleyn gave birth to a daughter, Elizabeth, Mary was made to serve as a lady-in-waiting to her half-sister. Anne hated Mary so strongly that she feared execution. Henry soon tired of Anne, however, and in 1536 she was put to death.

Mary became second in succession with the birth of Edward, Henry's son by his third wife, Jane Seymour. Mary became his godmother. Henry VIII died in 1547, and his nine-year-old son was crowned as Edward VI. Within five years he fell seriously ill, and a group of noblemen plotted to put Lady Jane Grey, a Protestant, on the throne. When Edward died in July 1553, Jane was recognized as queen, but the English considered Mary the rightful ruler. A few days later Mary made a triumphal entry into London and was welcomed as the new queen of England.

For a short time, Mary was popular with the people. She soon fell from favor, however, because of her desire to restore Roman Catholicism as England's state religion. To achieve this goal, she married Philip of Hapsburg, heir to the Spanish throne. The English disliked the marriage because they feared England might become a province of Roman Catholic Spain. The queen also revived old laws for punishing heretics, and some 300 Protestants suffered death by burning at the stake. The most notable martyr was Thomas Cranmer, archbishop of Canterbury, who had annulled Henry's marriage to Mary's mother.

Mary loved Philip, who was 11 years younger than she, but he neglected her. Philip left England in 1555 and became king of Spain in 1556. The next year he returned to England for a few months to persuade Mary to help Spain in a war against France. In the struggle England lost the seaport of Calais, which had been its outpost on the Continent since 1347.

In 1557, Mary became very ill; she died in London on November 17, 1558. She was succeeded by her Protestant half-sister Elizabeth I, daughter of Henry and Anne Boleyn.

CATHERINE DE MÉDICIS

(b. 1519–d. 1589)

Catherine de Médicis, queen consort of Henry II of France and subsequently regent of France, was one of the most influential personalities of the Catholic–Huguenot wars. Three of her sons were kings of France: Francis II, Charles IX, and Henry III.

Catherine was born April 13, 1519, in Florence, Italy. The daughter of Lorenzo di Piero de' Medici, duke of Urbino, and Madeleine de La Tour d'Auvergne, a Bourbon princess related to many of the French nobility, Catherine was highly educated, trained and disciplined by nuns in Florence and Rome. In 1533, she married Henry, duc d'Orléans, who later inherited the French crown from his father, Francis I; Catherine's uncle, Pope Clement VII, married the couple. Catherine bore 10 children, of whom four boys and three girls survived. She herself supervised their education.

Catherine was appointed regent in 1552 during Henry's absence at the siege of Metz. Upon the accidental death of her husband in

1559, Catherine was able to retain her power under her son, Francis II. Upon Francis's premature death on December 5, 1560, Catherine succeeded in obtaining the regency for her young son, Charles IX.

The 10 years from 1560 to 1570 were, politically, the most important of Catherine's life. They witnessed the first three civil wars and her desperate struggle against Catholic extremists for the independence of the crown and the maintenance of peace. In 1561, with the support of the distinguished chancellor Michel de L'Hospital, she began to effect reforms and economies by unassailably traditional methods, and to settle the religious conflict between Catholics and Protestants.

Trouble between the two religious factions was a basic element in the outbreak of civil war in 1562. Catherine ended the first civil war in March 1563 by the Edict of Amboise. In August 1563, she declared the king of age and, from April 1564 to January 1566, conducted him on a marathon itinerary round France. One principal purpose of the tour was to seek to strengthen peaceful relations between the crown and Spain, and to negotiate for Charles's marriage to Elizabeth of Austria.

During the period 1564–68, civil war broke out again. Catherine quickly terminated the second civil war with the Peace of Longjumeau, a renewal of Edict of Amboise. But she was unable to avert its revocation in 1568, which heralded the third civil war. She played a part in constructing the more far-reaching Treaty of Saint-Germain in 1570, which ended the third civil war.

For the next two years Catherine's policy was one of peace and general reconciliation. Then King Charles IX was urged to make war upon Spain in the Netherlands, which Catherine inevitably resisted. The issue of war or peace in the Netherlands was closely linked with the St. Bartholomew's Day massacre in Paris on Aug. 23–24, 1572, during which several thousand Huguenot Protestants were killed. Catherine traditionally has been blamed for these events, which have therefore fashioned the interpretation not only of her subsequent, but frequently also of her previous, career, resulting in the familiar myth of the wicked Italian queen.

Upon the death of Charles IX a year later, Catherine assumed the regency with the support of the parliament until the return from Poland of Henry III in August. Catherine placed high hopes in her favorite, Henry, for the regeneration of France, but not without simultaneous misgivings, knowing his weakness of character and his previous subjection to the Catholics. For these reasons Catherine neither sought to dominate Henry nor to rule in his place. Instead, much of her attention was devoted to restraining what she saw as his dangerous ambitions, which again threatened to involve France in hostilities with Spain.

In July 1586, at Henry's bidding, Catherine, though gravely ill undertook the arduous journey to see Navarre, the Protestant leader and heir presumptive, at Saint-Brice near Cognac. Despite the heroic efforts of Catherine's old age, France was sinking into chaos when she died at Blois on January 5, 1589, eight months before the murder of Henry III. Her ultimate achievement was to have saved the kingdom just long enough to ensure the succession of the Bourbon Henry IV, by whom the royal authority was restored.

GOLDA MEIR

(b. 1898–d. 1978)

One of the founders of the state of Israel, Golda Meir served in many posts in the Israeli government. She also served as prime minister from 1969 to 1974.

She was born Goldie Mabovitch in Kiev, Russia, on May 3, 1898. She and her family moved to Milwaukee, Wis., in 1906, and at 17 she joined the Zionist movement, which worked to establish a Jewish state in Palestine. In 1917, she married Morris Myerson, and they had two children. (She would adopt the Hebrew surname "Meir" at a later date.) The couple joined a kibbutz, or communal farm, in British-ruled Palestine in 1921.

Until the establishment of Israel, Golda Meir led missions to Europe and the United States for the World Zionist Organization and the Jewish

Agency for Palestine. She led resistance to the British and also worked with the British as a delegate to the Vaad Leumi, or National Council. The council was the chief organ of Jewish self-government under the British mandate.

During World War II, Meir served on the British War Economic Advisory Council. In May 1948, she was a signer of the declaration of independence of the new state of Israel. She became Israel's first ambassador to the Soviet Union in 1948, minister of labor in 1949, and foreign minister in 1956.

Meir retired in 1965, but was drafted as prime minister in 1969. She was returned to office after elections in 1969 and 1973. In the wake of a political crisis over setbacks in Israel's struggle for security, recognition, and peace in the Middle East, she resigned in 1974. She died in Jerusalem on Dec. 8, 1978.

RIGOBERTA MENCHÚ

(b. 1959–)

Rigoberta Menchú was a human rights activist in Guatemala. She was awarded the Nobel Peace Prize in 1992 for her efforts to achieve social justice for indigenous peoples and victims of government repression in her native country.

Menchú was born on Jan. 5, 1959, near San Marcos, Guatemala. A Mayan Indian of the Quiché group, she grew up in rural poverty and for a time worked as a domestic servant in Guatemala City. In 1981, after most of her family was killed by Guatemalan security forces, Menchú fled to Mexico, where she was cared for by members of a liberal Roman Catholic group. She soon joined international efforts to make the Guatemalan government cease its brutal counter-insurgency campaigns against Indian peasants. She became a skilled public speaker and organizer in the course of her efforts.

In 1983, Menchú gained international prominence with the publication of *I, Rigoberta Menchú*, a book based on recorded interviews that Menchú gave to anthropologist Elisabeth Burgos-Debray. The book—in which Menchú tells the story of her impoverished youth

Social activist Rigoberta Menchú, greeting supporters outside the Justice Palace in Guatemala City in April 2005, after the conviction of five Guatemalan politicians on charges of racial discrimination. © AP Images

and recounts in horrifying detail acts of violence perpetrated by government forces—was widely translated. After a controversy arose over the book's credibility, Menchú acknowledged that she had relied on both personal experience and the testimony of others in telling her story, but defended the work as an accurate portrayal of the sufferings of Guatemalan Indians.

With the money award she received from her Nobel Prize, Menchú established a foundation to help promote the rights of indigenous peoples worldwide. In 1993, she served as Goodwill Ambassador for the International Year of the Indigenous Peoples and later was a personal adviser to the general director of the United Nations Educational, Scientific and Cultural Organization.

MIRA BAI

(b. 1450?–d. 1547?)

Mira Bai was a was a Rajput princess who made a name for herself as a Hindu mystic and poet. Her lyrical songs of devotion to the god Krishna are widely popular in northern India.

Mira Bai was born in about 1450 in Kudaki, India. She was the only child of Ratan Singh, whose younger brother was the ruler of Merta. Her royal education included music and religion as well as instruction in politics and government. An image of Krishna given to her during childhood by a holy man began a lifetime of devotion to Krishna, whom she worshipped as her Divine Lover.

Mira Bai was married in 1516 to Bhoj Raj, crown prince of Mewar. Her husband died in 1521, probably of battle wounds, and thereafter she was the victim of much persecution and intrigue at the hands of her brother-in-law when he ascended the throne, and by his successor, Vikram Singh. Mira Bai was something of a rebel, and her religious pursuits did not fit the established pattern for a Rajput princess and widow. She spent most of her days in her private temple dedicated to Krishna, receiving sadhus (holy men) and pilgrims from throughout India and composing songs of devotion. At least two attempts made on her life are alluded to in her poems. Once a poisonous snake was sent to her in a basket of flowers, but when she opened it, she found an image of Krishna. On another occasion she was given a cup of poison but drank it without any harm.

Finally, Mira Bai left Mewar and returned to Merta, but finding that her unconventional behavior was not acceptable there either, she set out on a series of pilgrimages, eventually settling in Dwarka. In 1546, Udai Singh, who had succeeded Vikram Singh as Rana, sent a delegation of Brahmans to bring her back to Mewar. Reluctant, she asked permission to spend the night at the temple of Ranchorji (Krishna) and the next morning was found to have disappeared. According to popular belief, she miraculously merged with the image of Ranchorji, but whether she actually died that night or slipped away to spend the rest of her years wandering in disguise is not known.

Mira Bai belonged to a strong tradition of bhakti (devotional) poets in medieval India who expressed their love of God through the analogy of human relations—a mother's love for her child, a friend for a friend, or a woman for her beloved. The immense popularity and charm of her lyrics lies in their use of everyday images and in the sweetness of emotions easily understood by the people of India. It is believed she died in 1547 in Dwarka, Gujarat state, India.

MARIA MONTESSORI

(b. 1870–d. 1952)

A pioneer in modern education, Maria Montessori was an Italian psychiatrist who devised the progressive method that bears her name. She introduced her educational system, called the Montessori Method, in the early 1900s.

Maria Montessori was born on Aug. 31, 1870, near Ancona, Italy. In 1896, she became the first woman to be awarded a medical degree by the University of Rome. After graduation she worked with mentally challenged children. Her educational method developed from this work and from her experiences as director of Casa dei Bambini, or Children's House, a school for children.

The method is based on a child's natural development and growing awareness of the world as perceived through the senses. A variety of learning tools is provided, and the children themselves choose what they wish to use. The interest of the students is sustained by their feeling of accomplishment and by the pleasure derived from doing things they have chosen themselves. Among Montessori's best known books are *The Montessori Method*, published in 1912, and *The Secret of Childhood*, published in 1936.

In 1922, Montessori was appointed government inspector of schools. She left Italy in 1934 and spent time in Spain and in Ceylon (now Sri Lanka). She later moved to The Netherlands, where she died in Noordwijk aan Zee on May 6, 1952.

MOTHER TERESA

(b. 1910–d. 1997)

One of the most highly respected women in the world, Mother Teresa was internationally known for her charitable work among the victims of poverty and neglect—particularly in the slums of Calcutta (now Kolkata), India. In 1979, she was awarded the Nobel Peace Prize in recognition of her humanitarian efforts. She also received the Jewel of India, India's highest civilian medal, as well as honorary degrees from academic institutions worldwide.

Mother Teresa's original name was Agnes Gonxha Bojaxhiu. She was born in Skopje, Macedonia, of Albanian ancestry. She was baptized there on Aug. 27, 1910. At the age of 18 she decided to become a nun, and she ventured to Dublin, Ireland, to join the Sisters of Loretto, a community of Irish nuns with a mission in the Archdiocese of Calcutta. After a year she left Ireland to join the Loretto convent in Darjeeling, India. Her work included a teaching post at St. Mary's High School in Calcutta, where she witnessed the destitution that marked the city's slums. In 1946, Mother Teresa later recalled, she received a "call within a call," experiencing what she considered divine inspiration to begin a new chapter in her life, one devoted to helping the sick and impoverished. In that year she founded a new religious order, the Missionaries of Charity. This new order was officially recognized by the Roman Catholic Church in 1950. The order organized schools and opened centers to treat the blind, the aged, lepers, the disabled, and the dying. In 1952, Mother Teresa founded the Nirmal Hriday ("Place for the Pure of Heart") in Calcutta—a home to which terminally ill people could go to die with dignity. Despite her own religious beliefs, Mother Teresa demanded that the volunteers and workers at the Nirmal Hriday respect the religious beliefs of those who came for sanctuary in their last days. Under her guidance a leper colony called Shanti Nagar ("Town of Peace") was built near Asansol in West Bengal.

In the years after its inception, the Missionaries of Charity established centers throughout the world. In 1968, Pope Paul VI called

Mother Teresa to Rome to found a home there. In 1971, he awarded her the first Pope John XXIII Peace Prize. Under Mother Teresa's direction, the Missionaries of Charity established orphanages, nutrition centers, health care centers, and schools, bringing relief to diverse people, from impoverished blacks in South Africa to Christians and Muslims in war-torn Lebanon in the early 1980s to the poor in New York City's Harlem section.

After Mother Teresa suffered a heart attack in 1989, she was fitted with a pacemaker. Because of her health problems, she resigned as superior general of the order in April 1990. She was voted out of retirement by the members, however, and returned to her post in Sept. In early 1997, Mother Teresa began to suffer from increasingly severe health problems, including heart and kidney disorders. Only a few months after stepping down permanently from leadership of the Missionaries of Charity, she died of a heart attack in Calcutta on Sept. 5, 1997, at the age of 87. At that time, missions of Mother Teresa's order existed in more than 90 countries and had grown to include some 4,000 nuns and hundreds of thousands of lay workers and volunteers.

Within two years of her death, the process to declare her a saint was begun, with special authorization from Pope John Paul II. She was beatified on Oct. 19, 2003, reaching the ranks of the blessed in the shortest time in the history of the Roman Catholic Church.

MURASAKI SHIKIBU

(b. 978–d. 1014)

Murasaki Shikibu was born in 978, Kyōto, Japan. She was a court lady who was the author of the *Genji monogatari* (*The Tale of Genji*), generally considered the greatest work of Japanese literature and thought to be the world's oldest full novel.

The author's real name is unknown; it is believed that she acquired the sobriquet of Murasaki from the name of the heroine of her novel, and the name Shikibu reflects her father's position at the Bureau of Rites. She was born into a lesser branch of the noble and highly influential Fujiwara family and was well educated, having learned Chinese (generally

Painting depicting Murasaki Shikibu as she wrote her masterpiece, The Tale of the Genji.
Culture Club/Hulton Archive/Getty Images

the exclusive sphere of males). She married a much older distant cousin, Fujiwara Nobutaka, and bore him a daughter, but after two years of marriage he died.

Some critics believe that she wrote the entire *Tale of Genji* between 1001 (the year her husband died) and 1005, the year in which she was summoned to serve at court (for reasons unknown). It is more likely that the composition of her extremely long and complex novel extended over a much greater period; her new position within what was then a leading literary center likely enabled her to produce a story that was not finished until about 1010. In any case this work is the main source of knowledge about her life. It possesses considerable interest for the delightful glimpses it affords of life at the court of the empress Jōtō mon'in, whom Murasaki Shikibu served.

The Tale of Genji captures the image of a unique society of ultra-refined and elegant aristocrats, whose indispensable accomplishments were skill in poetry, music, calligraphy, and courtship. Much of it is concerned with the loves of Prince Genji and the different women in his life, all of whom are exquisitely delineated. Although the novel does not contain scenes of powerful action, it is permeated with sensitivity to human emotions and to the beauties of nature hardly paralleled elsewhere. The tone of the novel darkens as it progresses, indicating perhaps a deepening of Murasaki Shikibu's Buddhist conviction of the vanity of the world. Some, however, believe that its last 14 chapters were written by another author.

Shikibu died in 1014, in Kyōto, but her work lives on, having been translated a number of times over the years. The translation (1935) of *The Tale of Genji* by Arthur Waley is a classic of English literature. Murasaki Shikibu's diary is included in *Diaries of Court Ladies of Old Japan* (1935), translated by Annie Shepley Omori and Kochi Doi. Edward Seidensticker published a second translation of *The Tale of Genji* in 1976, and Royall Tyler translated a third in 2001.

NEFERTITI

(b. 1370 BCE–d. 1330 BCE)

Nefertiti was a queen of Egypt and the wife of King Akhenaton (formerly Amenhotep IV), who reigned from 1353 to 1336 BCE. Her name translates as "A Beautiful Woman Has Come." Nefertiti played a prominent role in the cult of the sun god known as the Aton.

Not much is known about Nefertiti's parentage, but early Egyptologists believed that she must have been a princess from Mitanni (Syria). Other evidence, however, suggests that she was the Egyptian-born daughter of the brother of Akhenaton's mother, which would make Nefertiti and Akhenaton cousins. It is known that Nefertiti had a younger sister and that she bore six daughters within 10 years of her marriage. Two of Nefertiti's daughters became queens of Egypt.

Most information on Nefertiti has been gathered from ancient images found in tombs and temples that were mostly uncovered in the early 20th century. The earliest pictures that were found come from tombs in Thebes; in these representations, Nefertiti is shown accompanying her husband. Other images depict her in a more prominent role, such as making offerings to the Aton or participating in the ritual killing of the female enemies of Egypt. In these images, Nefertiti wears her own unique headdress—a tall, straight-edged, flat-topped blue crown.

By the end of Akhenaton's fifth year as king, the Aton had become a major god in Egypt. The old state temples were closed and the court was transferred to a new capital city, Akhetaton (now called Tell el-Amarna). There Nefertiti continued to play an important religious role, serving in the divine trinity that she formed with the Aton and Akhenaton. Her sexuality, emphasized by her exaggeratedly feminine body shape and her fine linen garments, and her fertility, emphasized by the constant appearance of the six princesses, indicate that she was considered a living fertility goddess.

Soon after Akhenaton's 12th year as king, one of the princesses died, three other princesses disappeared (and are also presumed to have died), and Nefertiti vanished. The simplest explanation is that Nefertiti died, but there is no record of her death and no evidence that she was ever buried in the royal tomb at Akhetaton. Early Egyptologists deduced that Nefertiti had separated from Akhenaton and had moved to a different city, but this theory is now discredited. Others have suggested that she outlived her husband, took the name Smenkhkare, and ruled alone as female king before handing the throne to Tutankhamen. However, a male body identified in the 20th century as being Tutankhamen's brother makes it unlikely that Nefertiti and Smenkhkare were the same person. Nefertiti's body has not been discovered.

FLORENCE NIGHTINGALE

(b. 1820–d. 1910)

In 1954, the English nurse Florence Nightingale took a small band of volunteers to Turkey to care for soldiers wounded in the Crimean War. There she coped with conditions of crowding, poor sanitation, and shortage of basic supplies. After the war she established nursing as a profession and devoted the rest of her life to improving hospital care.

Nightingale was born on May 12, 1820, to well-to-do parents at their temporary residence in Florence, Italy. Named for her birthplace, she grew up in Derbyshire, Hampshire, and London, where her family maintained temporary homes. Nightingale was educated largely by her father. After her parents refused her request to study nursing at a hospital, Nightingale was persuaded to study parliamentary reports. In three years she was an expert on public health and hospitals.

Over her parents' objections she visited hospitals in England and continental Europe. In 1846, a friend sent her the Year Book of the Institution of Protestant Deaconesses at Kaiserswerth, Germany. Four years later Nightingale entered that same institution and was trained as a nurse. In 1853, she was appointed superintendent of the Institution for the Care of Sick Gentlewomen, in London.

Photographic portrait of Florence Nightingale, who is widely credited with the establishment of nursing as a medical profession. Images from the History of Medicine/National Library of Medicine/NIH

When war with Russia broke out, Nightingale volunteered her services. She was appointed head of the nurses in the military hospitals in Scutari, Turkey. When she arrived, more men were dying from fever and infection than from battle wounds. One of Nightingale's first requests was for scrubbing brushes. She enforced sanitary regulations, introduced special diets, and reduced the death rate from 45 to 2 percent. With her own money she bought linen, shirts, food, and even beds for the hospitals. Her health broke. She contracted Crimean fever and nearly died. But she refused to return to England.

By 1856, Florence Nightingale was world famous. She returned to England and met with Queen Victoria and other dignitaries to persuade them to improve conditions for the British soldier. From 1857 she lived as an invalid.

England gave her 50,000 pounds in 1860, which she used to establish the Nightingale School for Nurses. She campaigned by letter for hospital reforms, enforced high professional standards in caring for the sick, and established nursing as a respectable career for women. Nightingale died on Aug. 13, 1910, in London.

CHRISTIANE NÜSSLEIN-VOLHARD

(b. 1942–)

Nüsslein-Volhard, a German developmental geneticist was jointly awarded the 1995 Nobel Prize for Physiology or Medicine with geneticists Eric F. Wieschaus and Edward B. Lewis for their research concerning the mechanisms of early embryonic development. Nüsslein-Volhard, working in tandem with Wieschaus, expanded upon the pioneering work of Lewis, who used the fruit fly, or vinegar fly (*Drosophila melanogaster*), as an experimental subject. Her work has relevance to the development of all multicellular organisms, including humans.

Christiane Nüsslein-Volhard was born on Oct. 20, 1942, in Magdeburg, Germany. At Eberhard-Karl University of Tübingen, Nüsslein-Volhard received a diploma in biochemistry in 1968 and a doctorate in genetics in 1973. After holding fellowships in Basel and Freiburg, she joined Wieschaus as a group leader at the European Molecular Biology Laboratory in Heidelberg in 1978. In 1981, she returned to Tübingen, where, in 1985, she became director of the Max Planck Institute for Developmental Biology.

At Heidelberg, Nüsslein-Volhard and Wieschaus spent more than a year crossbreeding 40,000 fruit fly families and systematically examining their genetic makeup at a dual microscope. Their trial-and-error methods resulted in the discovery that of the fly's 20,000 genes, about 5,000 are deemed important to early development and about 140 are essential. They assigned responsibility for the fruit fly's embryonic development to three genetic categories: gap genes, which lay out the head-to-tail body plan; pair-rule genes, which determine body segmentation; and segment-polarity genes, which establish repeating structures within each segment.

In the early 1990s, Nüsslein-Volhard began studying genes that control development in the zebra fish *Danio rerio*. These organisms are ideal models for investigations into developmental biology because they have clear embryos, have a rapid rate of reproduction, and are closely related to other vertebrates. Nüsslein-Volhard studied the migration of cells from their sites of origin to their sites of destination within zebra fish embryos. Her investigations in zebra fish have helped elucidate genes and other cellular substances involved in human development and in the regulation of normal human physiology.

In addition to the Nobel Prize, Nüsslein-Volhard received the Leibniz Prize (1986) and the Albert Lasker Basic Medical Research Award (1991). She also published several books, including *Zebrafish: A Practical Approach* (2002; written with Ralf Dahm) and *Coming to Life: How Genes Drive Development* (2006).

SANDRA DAY O'CONNOR

(b. 1930–)

The first woman to be appointed an associate justice of the Supreme Court of the United States, Sandra Day O'Connor served from 1981 to until her retirement in 2006. A moderate conservative, she was known for her carefully researched opinions.

Sandra Day was born on March 26, 1930, in El Paso, Tex., but grew up on a large family ranch near Duncan, Ariz. She attended Stanford University, receiving an undergraduate degree in 1950 and a law degree in 1952. Upon her graduation she married a classmate, John Jay O'Connor III. Although she was highly qualified, she was unable to find employment in a law firm because she was a woman. After a brief tenure as a deputy district attorney in San Mateo County in California, she and her husband, a member of the U.S. Army Judge Advocate General Corps, moved to Germany, where she served as a civil attorney for the army from 1954 to 1957.

When O'Connor returned to the United States, she went into private practice in Maryville, Ariz., becoming an assistant attorney general for the state from 1965 to 1969. She subsequently served as a Republican member of the state Senate from 1969 until 1974 and eventually became the first female majority leader. In 1974, O'Connor was elected a Superior Court judge in Maricopa County, and five years later she was appointed to the Arizona Court of Appeals in Phoenix. President Ronald Reagan nominated her in July 1981 to fill the vacancy left on the Supreme Court by the retirement of Justice Potter Stewart. O'Connor was confirmed unanimously by the Senate and was sworn in as the first female justice in September.

O'Connor quickly became known for her practical approach and was considered a decisive swing vote in the Supreme Court's decisions. In such different fields as election law and abortion rights, she tried to create workable solutions to major constitutional questions, often over the course of several cases. O'Connor retired from the Supreme Court in 2006 and was replaced by Samuel A. Alito, Jr. In 2009, she received the U.S. Presidential Medal of Freedom.

OKUNI

(b. 1572?–d.?)

Okuni, also called Izumo no Okuni, was a Japanese dancer who is credited as being the founder of the Kabuki art form. Although many extant contemporary sources such as paintings, drawings, and diaries have shed light on Okuni's life, the accuracy of such primary sources has been difficult to establish.

Very little is known about Okuni's life for certain. She is said to have been an attendant at the Grand Shrine of Izumo, the oldest Shintō shrine in Japan. It is possible that she was a temple dancer or even a prostitute. She formed a troupe of female dancers who in 1603 gave a highly popular performance of dances and light sketches on a makeshift stage set up in the dry bed of the Kamo River in Kyōto. The performance was a strong departure from the older, traditional Noh drama style, in which the actors engaged in slow, deliberate movements. It was so popular that she arranged a variety of other similar events. According to some accounts, Okuni dressed as a young man while she performed certain dances. The company's lusty and unrestrained dance dramas soon became known throughout Japan—the style acquiring the name Okuni Kabuki—and other troupes of female dancers were formed.

Okuni's company and the newer groups normally had the patronage of the nobility, but their appeal was directed toward ordinary townspeople, and the themes of their dramas and dances were taken from everyday life. The popularity of onna ("women's") Kabuki remained high until women's participation was officially banned in 1629 by the shogun (military ruler) Tokugawa Iemitsu, who thought that the sensuality of the dances had a deleterious effect on public morality. Not only were the dances considered suggestive, but the dancers themselves earned extra money by means of prostitution. The ban on women performing Kabuki lasted until the Meiji Restoration in 1868. For a time, as in Elizabethan theatre, boys and young men performed the female roles while dressed as women. In 1652, their involvement was also banned by the shogun for moral reasons. Older male dancers subsequently took over these roles.

Ariyoshi Sawako's work of fiction *Izumo no Okuni* (1969; *Kabuki Dancer*) is an imagined biography of Okuni that provides an enlightened look at 16th- and 17th-century Japanese culture.

EMMELINE PANKHURST

(b. 1858–d. 1928)

Pankhurst was a British militant suffrage leader who fought for 40 years to achieve equal voting rights for men and women in England. Her daughter Christabel Harriette Pankhurst (1880–1958) also was prominent in the woman suffrage movement.

Emmeline Goulden was born on July 14, 1858, in Manchester, England. She married Richard Marsden Pankhurst in 1879. He was a prominent lawyer and the author of the first woman suffrage bill in Great Britain and of the Married Women's Property Acts of 1870 and 1882. In 1889, she founded the Women's Franchise League, which won for married women the right to vote in elections to local offices. From 1895, she held a succession of municipal offices in Manchester. There in 1903 she cofounded with Christabel the Women's Social and Political

Union (WSPU). The organization gained widespread attention two years later when Christabel and another member, Annie Kenney, were arrested for assault on the police and, after having refused to pay fines, were sent to prison.

From 1906, Emmeline Pankhurst directed WSPU activities from London. She believed that the ruling Liberal government was preventing woman suffrage, so she campaigned against the party's candidates at elections. Her followers joined the fray by interrupting meetings of Cabinet ministers. In 1908–09, Pankhurst was jailed three times. She declared a truce in 1910, but it was broken when the government blocked a "conciliation" bill on woman suffrage. Beginning in July 1912, the WSPU turned to extreme militancy, mainly in the form of arson directed by Christabel from Paris, where she had gone to avoid arrest for conspiracy. Pankhurst herself was arrested, released, and rearrested 12 times within a year under an act that let hunger-striking prisoners free for a time to regain their health before being re-incarcerated. When World War I started in 1914, she and Christabel called off the suffrage campaign, and the government released all suffragist prisoners. Pankhurst's autobiography, *My Own Story*, appeared that same year.

Previously to the war, Pankhurst had made three trips to the United States to lecture on woman suffrage. She returned during the war years, visiting the United States, Canada, and Russia to encourage the industrial mobilization of women. Pankhurst lived in the United States, Canada, and Bermuda until 1926, when she returned to England. There she was chosen Conservative candidate for an east London constituency, but her health failed before she could be elected. The Representation of the People Act of 1928, giving equal suffrage to men and women, was passed a few weeks before her death, which occurred on June 14, 1928, in London.

ROSA PARKS

(b. 1913–d. 2005)

By refusing to give up her bus seat to a white man in the segregated South, Rosa Parks sparked the United States civil rights movement.

Civil rights activist Rosa Parks, standing next to a portrait of herself depicting the moment she would not give up her bus seat, in 1990. Time & Life Pictures/Getty Images

Her action led to the 1955–56 Montgomery, Ala., bus boycott, and she became a symbol of the power of nonviolent protest.

Rosa Louise McCauley was born on Feb. 4, 1913, in Tuskegee, Ala. She briefly attended Alabama State Teachers College (now Alabama State University) and in 1932 married Raymond Parks, a barber. She worked as a seamstress and became active in the National Association for the Advancement of Colored People (NAACP), serving as secretary of the Montgomery chapter from 1943 to 1956.

On her way home from work one day in 1955, Parks was told by a bus driver to surrender her seat to a white man. When she refused, she was arrested and fined, an action that motivated local black leaders to take action. Emerging civil rights leader Martin Luther King,

Jr., led a boycott of the bus company that lasted more than a year. In 1956, the U.S. Supreme Court upheld a lower court's decision declaring Montgomery's segregated bus seating unconstitutional.

Parks moved to Detroit, Mich., in 1957. She worked in the office of Michigan congressman John Conyers, Jr., from 1965 until she retired in 1988. She remained active in the NAACP and other civil rights groups. The Southern Christian Leadership Conference established the Rosa Parks Freedom Award in her honor, and in 1979, the NAACP awarded her its Spingarn Medal. In 1987 she cofounded an institute to help educate young people and teach them leadership skills. An autobiography, *Rosa Parks: My Story*, appeared in 1992. She was the recipient of two of the U.S. government's most prestigious civilian honors—the Presidential Medal of Freedom (1996) and the Congressional Gold Medal of Honor (1999)—for her contributions to the civil rights movement. Parks died on Oct. 24, 2005, in Detroit.

ANNA PAVLOVA

(b. 1881–d. 1931)

Enchanted audiences the world over thought that "Pavlova does not dance; she soars as though on wings." No dancer worked harder to perfect her art. Even at the height of her fame, the small, slender dancer practiced 15 hours a day.

Anna Pavlovna Pavlova was born on Feb. 12, 1881 (January 31 according to the calendar being used at the time), in St. Petersburg, Russia. When Pavlova was 8 years old, her mother took her to a performance of Tchaikovsky's ballet *The Sleeping Beauty*. After seeing this performance she decided to become a dancer. She entered the Imperial Ballet School in 1891. After years of hard work and discipline, she graduated. In 1899 she joined the Imperial Ballet, and in 1906, she became prima ballerina. In 1907 and 1908, she joined a group of dancers and toured Stockholm, Sweden; Copenhagen, Denmark; and other European cities.

In 1909, Sergei Diaghilev presented a season of Russian ballet in Paris, France, and Pavlova appeared there with his company.

Russian dancer Anna Pavlova, rehearsing with partner Alexandre Volsinine for a 1926 performance in London. Topical Press Agency/Hulton Archive/Getty Images

A short time later she undertook a series of independent tours in which she introduced classical ballet throughout the world. She became interested in the traditional dance techniques of other countries, including India and Japan, and the world became her home. Although she owned a country estate in England, at Hampstead Heath, near London, she spent little time there. She and her manager and accompanist, Victor Dandré, were married in 1914, but she kept their marriage secret for years.

Among the many dances associated with Pavlova are *Coppélia*, in which she made her American debut at the Metropolitan Opera House in 1910, *Autumn Leaves*, *Les Sylphides*, and *Glow Worm*. Most beloved of all was *The Dying Swan*, arranged for her by Michel Fokine. She died on Jan. 23, 1931, in The Hague, The Netherlands.

EVA PERÓN

(b. 1919–d. 1952)

Eva Perón helped lead the populist government of her husband, Argentine President Juan Perón, in the 1940s and 1950s. Both reviled and adored by different factions, many observers claimed that she exploited the people she claimed to represent and at the same time, she did, to an extent, serve the working classes of her country by positioning herself as a bridge between the government and the laborers.

María Eva Ibarguren was born to Juana Ibarguren on May 7, 1919, outside the small town of Los Toldos on the Argentine pampas. Her father, Juan Duarte, was married to another woman and would not allow the child to bear his family name. Her mother, Juana, took her children to the town of Junín six years later.

Eva wanted to become an actress, and when she was only 15 she traveled by herself to the capital, Buenos Aires. She managed to find work and was performing steadily in radio parts by the time she was 20. Calling herself Eva Duarte, the young actress began to attract attention from the public and from a rising star of the new government, Col. Juan Domingo Perón. They met in 1943. Political unrest led to the arrest of Juan Perón, then vice president of the republic, in October 1945. In a massive demonstration the working people demanded the return of their leader. Shortly thereafter, Perón was released and he and Eva soon married. Perón won the presidency in 1946.

Eva, or Evita as she was popularly known, immediately began to make her presence felt. She took over her husband's role as caretaker of the working classes. She assisted in the creation of her image by purchasing the newspaper *Democracia*. She also formed the Eva Perón Foundation, a charitable organization for the poor that grew to be her major vehicle for implementing social programs and reforms.

In the summer of 1947, Eva Perón left for a tour of Europe, beginning with a meeting with Francisco Franco, the fascist leader of Spain.

Her association with Franco and her own husband's military-populist regime led to a lukewarm reception in much of post–World War II Europe. Upon her return from this trip, she again took up her causes. In 1948, she helped complete a housing project, installed drinking water facilities, opened a transitional home for women, and worked to improve the education and living conditions of the country's poor. Through the Eva Perón Foundation, she created more than 1,000 new schools. Although some criticized her for questionable use of funds and for crowding out other charitable efforts, to "her people" Evita was evolving from the image of a generous mother into that of a saint and a martyr.

In mid-1949, the Perónist Women's Party was formed, with Eva Perón as president. She also began to act as a strike negotiator. Her influence extended to all branches of the government, and the line between her husband's power and her own was increasingly blurry. She made this fact palatable to her public by tying all her accomplishments to her husband's "great work." By continually pledging herself to him and to the laborers, she created the illusion that it was they, not she, who wielded her substantial power.

All the while Eva Perón had been secretly fighting cancer. She continued to take on more responsibilities against her doctors' warnings. In 1950, she underwent a hysterectomy and forced a quick recovery. On Aug. 22, 1950, a renomination ceremony for Juan Perón was held, during which the crowd called for Eva to run as vice president. She declined the nomination, a decision that surprised even those closest to her.

Eva Perón wrote her autobiography, *La Razón de Mi Vida* (*The Reason for My Life*), while confined to a sickbed. She died on July 26, 1952, at the age of 33. A continual stream of mourners viewed her remains for weeks, sometimes forming lines 35 blocks long. For the next 22 years, her body was passed from place to place—including to Madrid and back—in a bizarre series of attempts by her husband and his enemies to capitalize on her power. She was supposedly buried in Buenos Aires in November 1974, but the question of her final resting place was never definitively answered.

MARY ROBINSON

(b. 1944–)

Irish lawyer, politician, and diplomat Mary Robinson served as Ireland's first woman president from 1990 to 1997. She was then the United Nations High Commissioner for Human Rights from 1997 to 2002. She was born Mary Teresa Winifred Bourke on May 21, 1944, in Ballina, County Mayo, Ireland.

Robinson attended Trinity College and King's Inns in Dublin and Harvard University in the United States. She joined Trinity's law faculty as the youngest professor in the school's history. From 1969 to 1989, she was a member of the Senate. She was elected to the Royal Irish Academy and was a member of the International Commission of Jurists in Geneva from 1987 to 1990. She was also a member of the Dublin City Council from 1979 to 1983 and ran unsuccessfully in 1977 and 1981 for Dublin parliamentary constituencies.

Robinson became Ireland's president in 1990. She was strongly committed to human rights and was an advocate of divorce, contraceptives, and homosexuality. Shortly before her term as president ended, she took up the post of United Nations High Commissioner for Human Rights. In that position, she emphasized the promotion of human rights at the national and regional levels. She left office in 2002 but remained active in nongovernmental posts. In 2009, she received the U.S. Presidential Medal of Freedom.

ELEANOR ROOSEVELT

(b. 1884–d. 1962)

The wife of U.S. President Franklin D. Roosevelt, Eleanor Roosevelt was a great reformer and humanitarian who strove to improve the lives of people all over the world. Her defense of the rights of minorities, youth, women, and the poor during her tenure as First Lady of the United States helped to shed light on groups that previously had been alienated from the political process. After her husband's death, as a delegate to the United Nations, she helped write the Universal Declaration of Human Rights (1948).

Anna Eleanor Roosevelt was born in New York City on Oct. 11, 1884. Her uncle, Theodore Roosevelt, later became 26th president of the United States. Eleanor grew up in a wealthy family that attached great value to community service. Both her parents and a brother died before she was 10, and Eleanor and her surviving brother were raised by their strict grandmother. The death of Eleanor's father, to whom she had been especially close, was very difficult for her.

Eleanor Roosevelt (left) *receiving a Red Cross pin from an unidentified worker on the White House grounds during Roosevelt's tenure as First Lady.* Library of Congress Prints & Photographs Division

Relatives hoped to polish 15-year-old Eleanor—a girl considered sweet but plain and awkward—by enrolling her at Allenswood, a girls' boarding school outside London. There she came under the influence of the French headmistress Marie Souvestre, whose intellectual curiosity and taste for travel and excellence awakened similar interests in Eleanor, who later described her three years there as the happiest time of her life. Reluctantly, Eleanor returned to New York in the summer of 1902 to prepare for her debut into society that winter. Following family tradition, she devoted time to community service, including teaching in a settlement house on Manhattan's Lower East Side.

Soon after Eleanor returned to New York, Franklin Roosevelt, her distant cousin, began to court her. Despite the objections of his mother, with whom Eleanor continued to have problems throughout her married life, the couple wed on March 17, 1905, in New York City, with Uncle Theodore (then president) giving away the bride. Between 1906 and 1916, Eleanor gave birth to five healthy children—Anna, James, Elliott, Franklin, Jr., and John—and another son who died in infancy.

After Franklin Roosevelt won a seat in the New York Senate in 1911, the family moved to Albany, where Eleanor was initiated into the job of political wife. When Franklin was appointed Assistant Secretary of the Navy in 1913, the family moved to Washington, D.C., and Eleanor spent the next few years performing expected social duties. With the entry of the United States into World War I in April 1917, Eleanor was able to resume her volunteer work. She visited wounded soldiers and worked for the Navy-Marine Corps Relief Society and in a Red Cross canteen.

Franklin ran unsuccessfully for vice president on the Democratic ticket in 1920. At this time Eleanor's interest in politics increased, partly as a result of her decision to help in her husband's political career after he was stricken with poliomyelitis in 1921 and partly as a result of her desire to work for important causes. She joined the Women's Trade Union League and became active in the New York state Democratic Party. As a member of the Legislative Affairs Committee of the League of Women Voters, she began studying the Congressional Record and learned to evaluate voting records and debates.

When Franklin became governor of New York in 1929, Eleanor found an opportunity to combine the responsibilities of a political hostess with her own burgeoning career and personal independence. She continued to teach at Todhunter, girls' school in Manhattan that she and two friends had purchased, making several trips a week back and forth between Albany and New York City.

Entering the White House during the Great Depression, Mrs. Roosevelt helped to plan work camps for girls, to establish the National Youth Administration in 1935, and to launch projects to employ writers, artists, musicians, and actors. She insisted that women's wages be equal to men's. Throughout the 1930s, she supported Arthurdale, an experimental homestead community for destitute mining families in West Virginia.

Eleanor instituted regular White House press conferences for women correspondents, and wire services that had not formerly employed women were forced to do so in order to have a representative present. In deference to the president's disability, she helped serve as his "eyes and ears" throughout the nation, embarking on extensive tours and reporting to him on conditions, programs, and public opinion. Beginning in 1936 she wrote a daily syndicated newspaper column, "My Day," and she also gave frequent radio talks. A widely sought-after speaker at political meetings and at various institutions, she showed particular interest in child welfare, housing reform, and equal rights for women and racial minorities.

In 1939, when the Daughters of the American Revolution (DAR) refused to let Marian Anderson, an African American opera singer, perform in Constitution Hall, Eleanor resigned her membership in the DAR and arranged to hold the concert at the nearby Lincoln Memorial. The event turned into a massive outdoor celebration attended by 75,000 people. On another occasion, when local officials in Alabama insisted that seating at a public meeting be segregated by race, Eleanor carried a folding chair to all sessions and carefully placed it in the center aisle. She also was concerned about the improvement of health and education on Indian reservations and fought for the preservation of Native American culture.

After her husband's death on April 12, 1945, Eleanor made plans to retire, but she did not keep them. President Harry S. Truman appointed her a delegate to the United Nations (UN), where she served as chairman of the Commission on Human Rights (1946–51) and played a major role in the drafting and adoption of the Universal Declaration of Human Rights. In the 1950s, she toured India, Pakistan, the Middle East, and the Soviet Union, investigating social conditions and discussing the problems of world peace. In the United States, Eleanor worked for the election of Democratic presidential candidates and supported social welfare legislation. In 1961, President John F. Kennedy appointed her chairman of his Commission on the Status of Women

Eleanor was diagnosed with a rare form of tuberculosis. She died on Nov. 7, 1962, in New York City. She was buried at Hyde Park, her husband's family home on the Hudson River and the site of the Franklin D. Roosevelt Library.

SACAGAWEA

(b. 1788–d. 1812)

A teenager named Sacagawea served as an interpreter for the Lewis and Clark Expedition to the western United States. A Lemhi Shoshone Indian, she traveled thousands of miles through the wilderness with the explorers, from the Dakotas to the Pacific Ocean and back again. Many memorials have been raised in her honor, in part for the fortitude with which she faced hardship on the difficult journey.

Separating fact from legend in Sacagawea's life is difficult. Historians disagree on the dates of her birth and death and even on her name. One version of her name, Sacagawea, means "Bird Woman" in the Hidatsa language. Alternatively, her name is sometimes spelled Sacajawea or Sakakawea. She is thought to have been born in about 1788, near the Continental Divide at what is now the Idaho-Montana border. In about 1800, when she was about 12 years old, a raiding party of Hidatsa Indians captured her near the headwaters of the Missouri River. The Hidatsa made her a slave and took her to the Mandan-Hidatsa villages near what is now Bismarck, N.D. In about 1804, she became one of the wives of the French Canadian fur trader Toussaint Charbonneau. (Sacagawea may have been sold to him.)

The explorers Meriwether Lewis and William Clark arrived at the Mandan-Hidatsa villages and built a fort there in which to spend the winter. They hired Charbonneau as an interpreter to help them speak with the various Indian peoples they would encounter on their expedition. However, he did not speak Shoshone. The expedition would need to communicate with the Shoshone to acquire horses to use to cross the mountains. For this reason, the explorers agreed that the pregnant Sacagawea should also accompany them. On Feb. 11, 1805, she gave birth to a son, Jean Baptiste.

Sacagawea took her infant along on the expedition, which set off on April 7 on the Missouri River. On May 14, Charbonneau nearly capsized the dugout boat in which Sacagawea was riding. Remaining calm, she retrieved important papers, instruments, medicine, and other valuables that otherwise would have been lost. Sacagawea also proved to be a significant asset in other ways, such as in searching for edible plants and in making moccasins and clothing. She also helped allay the suspicions of approaching Indian tribes through her presence—a woman and child accompanying a party of men indicated peaceful intentions.

By mid-August the expedition encountered a band of Shoshone. Their leader was Sacagawea's brother Cameahwait. The reunion of Sacagawea and her brother helped Lewis and Clark obtain the horses and guide that enabled them to cross the Rocky Mountains.

Sacagawea was not the guide for the expedition, as some have wrongly portrayed her. She did, however, recognize landmarks in southwestern Montana. She also informed Clark that Bozeman Pass was the best route between the Missouri and Yellowstone rivers on their return journey. Sacagawea and her family left the expedition when they arrived back at the Mandan-Hidatsa villages.

It is believed that Sacagawea died shortly after giving birth to a daughter, Lisette, on Dec. 20, 1812, at Fort Manuel, near what is now Mobridge, S.D. Clark became the legal guardian of her two children.

In the years since her death, Sacagawea has become a legend, the subject of many books and movies. She has also been honored with monuments, statues, U.S. postage stamps, and a U.S. dollar coin. In 2001, she was given the title of honorary sergeant in the regular U.S. Army.

MARGARET SANGER

(b. 1883–d. 1966)

Margaret Sanger was the founder of the birth control movement in the United States, a nurse who worked among the poor on the Lower East Side of New York City. There she witnessed first-hand the results of uncontrolled fertility, self-induced abortions, and high rates of infant and maternal mortality.

Margaret Sanger was born Margaret Higgins in Corning, N.Y., on Sept. 14, 1883. She took her nurse's training at the White Plains

Hospital and the Manhattan Eye and Ear Clinic. She married William Sanger in 1900. Although she later divorced him, she kept the last name by which she had become well known, even after she remarried in 1922.

Sanger believed in a woman's right to plan the size of her family. In 1912, she gave up nursing to devote herself full-time to the cause of birth control. In 1914, she founded the National Birth Control League and in that same year was indicted for sending out copies of the periodical *The Woman Rebel*, which advocated birth control. At that time the federal Comstock Law of 1873 classified such literature as obscene. Her case was dismissed in 1916. Later that year she opened the first birth control clinic in the United States in Brooklyn, N.Y. She was arrested and served 20 days in jail in 1917 for creating a public nuisance. Continued government harassment brought public opinion to her side, and in 1936 the 1873, the law was modified.

In 1921, Sanger founded the American Birth Control League and served as its president until 1928. That and later organizations became in 1942 the Planned Parenthood Federation of America. Sanger organized the first World Population Conference in Geneva, Switzerland, in 1927 and was also the first president of the International Planned Parenthood Federation, organized in 1953. She helped promote family planning in India and Japan. She wrote several books, including *My Fight for Birth Control* (1931). Sanger died in Tucson, Ariz., on Sept. 6, 1966.

SAPPHO

(b. 610 BCE–d. 580 BCE)

S appho was one of the best lyric poets of ancient Greece. She ranks with Archilochus and Alcaeus, among Greek poets, for her ability to impress readers with a lively sense of her personality. Unfortunately nearly all of her works have been lost; except for one work, only fragments have survived.

The exact dates of her birth and death are unknown, but Sappho flourished from about 610 to 580 BCE. She lived most of her life in

Mytilene on the island of Lesbos, and she is reputed to have married Cercolas from the island of Andros.

The themes of her poems are personal, concerning friendships with and hostility toward other women. Her brother Charaxus was also the subject of several poems. She wrote about the loves, hates, and jealousies that flourished among the wealthy women who often met together in associations to spend their days composing poetry and other relaxations.

Sappho's poems probably circulated in her lifetime. They were collected during the 3rd or 2nd century BCE and published in ten books. This edition did not survive the Middle Ages. By the 8th or 9th century CE she was represented only by quotations in the works of other authors. Her only surviving complete poem is 28 lines long.

Legends about Sappho abound, including one about her death. Most modern critics consider it legend that Sappho leaped from a cliff to certain death in the sea because of her unrequited love of Phaon, a younger man and a sailor.

SOONG MEI-LING

(b. 1897–d. 2003)

Fresco of a woman believed to be the ancient Greek poet Sappho. Mondadori Portfolio/ Getty Images

Soong Mei-ling greatly influenced politics in China and later Taiwan. She was the second wife of the Nationalist Chinese president Chiang Kai-shek

The fourth child of Charlie Soong, she was born on March 5, 1897, in Shanghai. She spent several years attending schools in the United States. By the time she graduated from Wellesley College in 1917, she was thoroughly Americanized. After marrying Chiang Kai-shek in 1927, she helped introduce him to Western ways and promoted his cause in the West.

Soong became very well admired in the United States. During World War II, she wrote many articles about China for American journals. On a visit to the United States in 1943, she sought and received from the U.S. Congress increased funding to support China in its war with Japan. She became the first Chinese person and the second woman to address a joint session of Congress.

Civil war broke out in China in the 1940s, as Chiang's Nationalists fought the communists for control of the country. When the Nationalists were defeated in 1949, Chiang transplanted his government to Taiwan. Soong, who joined her husband on the island, remained highly influential. She helped to sway the U.S. position toward supporting the government of Taiwan for many years. After Chiang's death in 1975, Soong moved to New York City. She died there on Oct. 23, 2003.

GERMAINE DE STAEL

(b. 1766–d. 1817)

After the French Revolution the gatherings arranged by Madame de Staël in Switzerland and France attracted Europe's intellectuals. She had developed her curiosity, wit, and other conversational charms as a child in her mother's salon, and her influence on Romanticism brought her fame in her 20s. Critics called two of her multivolume 19th-century novels, *Delphine* and *Corinne*, the first modern feminist, psychological romances.

Anne-Louise-Germaine Necker was born in Paris on April 22, 1766. Her father was Louis XVI's finance minister. In 1786, she married Baron Erik de Staël-Holstein, the Swedish ambassador to France. She soon became known for her essays on Jean-Jacques Rousseau in which she advocated a moderate constitutional monarchy as a solution to the French political crisis. In 1793, she fled the Reign of Terror for her family home in Coppet, Switzerland, where she entertained prominent literary and political figures until her return to Paris the next year.

De Staël set forth the principles of a new literary theory in such essays as "A Treatise on the Influence of the Passions upon the Happiness of Individuals and of Nations" (1796). Because of the liberal viewpoint that she represented and her friendship with revolutionaries, she was banished by Napoleon Bonaparte in 1803. He later banned her *Germany*, a three-volume critical study, as an anti-French work. After ten years in exile she returned to Paris, where she died on July 14, 1817.

GERTRUDE STEIN

(b. 1874–d. 1946)

Although she fancied herself a genius and published a number of books and plays, Gertrude Stein is remembered best for the talented people who visited her in Paris, France. She and her brother, art critic Leo Stein, were among the first to appreciate and collect the works of such major artists as Pablo Picasso, Paul Cézanne, and Henri Matisse. She also befriended and encouraged such expatriate American writers as Ernest Hemingway and Sherwood Anderson.

Stein was born on Feb. 3, 1874, in Allegheny, Pa. She grew up in Oakland, Calif., and attended Radcliffe College (graduated in 1898)

Gertrude Stein, relaxing on the sofa of her Paris studio. Above and to the right is a portrait of Stein painted by Pablo Picasso. Library of Congress Prints & Photographs Division

in Cambridge, Massachusetts, and, for a time, the medical school at Johns Hopkins University in Baltimore, Maryland. In 1903, she joined her brother in Paris. Except for time spent in the French village of Culoz during World War II, Paris was her home for the rest of her life.

Stein and her brother were among the first collectors of works by the Cubists and other experimental painters of the period, such as Pablo Picasso (who painted her portrait), Henri Matisse, and Georges Braque, several of whom became her friends. At her salon they mingled with expatriate American writers whom she dubbed the "Lost Generation," including Sherwood Anderson and Ernest Hemingway, and other visitors drawn by her literary reputation. Her literary and artistic judgments were revered, and her chance remarks could make or destroy reputations.

Stein's first book, *Three Lives*, was published in 1909 and describes the lives of three working-class women. Her best-known book is *The Autobiography of Alice B. Toklas* (1933). Although the name in the title is that of Stein's friend and companion for many years, the book is by and about Stein herself. Toklas's actual autobiography, *What Is Remembered* (1963), appeared long after Stein's death. Stein also wrote the librettos for two operas by Virgil Thomson—*Four Saints in Three Acts* (1934) and *The Mother of Us All* (1947). Her last book, *Brewsie and Willie* (1946), is about the American servicemen who visited her during the war. Stein died on July 27, 1946, in Paris.

ELIZABETH STERN

(b. 1915–d. 1980)

E lizabeth Stern was a Canadian-born American pathologist, or a doctor who specializes in finding out how disease affects the human body. She was noted for her work on the stages of a cell's progression from a normal to a cancerous state.

Elizabeth Stern Shankman was born on Sept. 19, 1915, Cobalt, Ontario, Canada. She received a medical degree from the University of Toronto in 1939 and the following year went to the United States, where she became a naturalized citizen in 1943. She received further medical training at the Pennsylvania Medical School and at the Good Samaritan and Cedars of Lebanon hospitals in Los Angeles. She was one of the first specialists in cytopathology, the study of diseased cells. From 1963, she was professor of epidemiology (tracking of and controlling disease within a population) in the School of Public Health at the University of California, Los Angeles.

While at UCLA, Stern became interested in cervical cancer, and she began to focus her research solely on its causes and progression. The discoveries she made during this period led her to publish in 1963 what is believed to be the first case report linking a specific virus (herpes simplex virus) to a specific cancer (cervical cancer). For another phase of her research she studied a group of more than 10,000 Los Angeles county women who were clients of the county's public family planning clinics. In a 1973 article in the journal *Science*, Stern became the first person to report a definite link between the prolonged use of oral contraceptives and cervical cancer. Her research connected the use of contraceptive pills containing steroids with cervical dysplasia, which is often a precursor of cervical cancer. In her most noted work in this field, Stern studied cells cast off from the lining of the cervix and discovered that a normal cell goes through 250 distinct stages of cell progression before reaching an advanced stage of cervical cancer. This prompted the development of diagnostic techniques and screening instruments to detect the cancer in its early stages. Her research helped make cervical cancer, with its slow rate of metastasis, one of the types of cancer that can be successfully treated by prophylactic measures (i.e., excision of abnormal tissue).

Stern continued her teaching and research into the late 1970s, despite undergoing chemotherapy for stomach cancer. She died of the disease on Aug. 19, 1980, in Los Angeles.

MARTHA STEWART

(b. 1941–)

Martha Stewart is an American entrepreneur and domestic lifestyle innovator. She is known for building a catering business into an international media and home-furnishing corporation, Martha Stewart Living Omnimedia, Inc.

Martha Stewart, née Martha Helen Kostyra was born on Aug. 3, 1941, in Jersey City, N.J. Raised in Nutley, N.J., Stewart grew up in a Polish American household where the traditional arts of cooking, sewing, canning and preserving, housekeeping, and gardening were practiced. She started planning birthday parties for neighbor children while she was in grammar school, and she paid her college tuition by taking modeling jobs in New York City. She married law student Andrew Stewart (1961; they divorced in 1990) while studying at Barnard College. Their daughter, Alexis, was born in 1965.

Stewart worked as a stockbroker at a small Wall Street firm (1965–72) until she and her family moved to Westport, Connecticut, and turned their ambitions toward restoring Turkey Hill, a Federal-style farmhouse. There they gardened, restored, and decorated, acquiring the skills and the setting for books and TV shows.

After launching a catering business in 1976 with a partner, Norma Collier, Stewart's talent for innovation and presentation attracted a string of prestigious clients. Her first book, *Entertaining* (1982; written with Elizabeth Hawes), set the tone for subsequent publications: superb art direction, gorgeous settings, labor-intensive recipes, and decorating projects. In addition, she oversaw the CBS Masterworks Dinner Classics, a series of music compilations that could provide the appropriate background music for a variety of meals and gatherings.

Following continued success with such books as *Martha Stewart's Hors d'Oeuvres* (1984) and *Weddings* (1987), Time Publishing Ventures, Inc., teamed with Stewart (1990) to publish a monthly magazine, *Martha Stewart Living*, with Stewart not only as editor in chief but as the featured personality within its pages. She began a syndicated television show of the same name (1993–2004) and eventually bought the magazine from Time Warner, Inc. (1997), funding the purchase with proceeds from her merchandising arrangement with Kmart, which debuted as the Martha Stewart Everyday line of household furnishings.

Each of these business moves took her closer to her ultimate goal of creating a multichannel media and marketing firm. That goal was fully realized when Martha Stewart Living Omnimedia was listed on the

New York Stock Exchange (1999), with Stewart as chairman and chief executive officer (CEO). She became a billionaire, however briefly, with the public launch of her company, although the company struggled to turn a profit during the following decade.

In December 2001, Stewart was accused of insider trading. She stepped down as chairman and CEO of her firm in 2003, assuming the title of chief creative officer, while defending herself against charges of lying and obstructing justice. After being convicted in 2004, she retained only an editorial role with the company. Stewart served five months in prison followed by five months of home detention, during which she urged her fans to continue supporting her business.

She returned to daytime television with *Martha* (2005–12), and in 2010, she was appointed chief editorial, media, and content officer of Martha Stewart Living Omnimedia. The following year, upon the expiration of a ban imposed by the Securities and Exchange Commission as part of a 2006 settlement on the insider trading conviction, she rejoined the company's board. In 2012, she resumed her duties as chairman.

MARIE STOPES

(b. 1880–d. 1958)

Scottish botanist and birth control advocate Marie Stopes founded the United Kingdom's first instructional clinic for contraception. Although her clinical work, writings, and speeches evoked violent opposition, especially from Roman Catholics, she greatly influenced the Church of England's gradual relaxation (from 1930) of its stand against birth control.

Marie Charlotte Carmichael Stopes was born on Oct. 15, 1880, in Edinburgh. She grew up in a wealthy, educated family; her father was an architect, her mother a scholar of Shakespeare and an advocate for the education of women. Stopes obtained a science degree (1902) from University College, London, which she completed in only two years. She went on to do postgraduate studies in paleobotany (fossil plants), earning a doctorate from the University of Munich in 1904. That same year she became an assistant lecturer of botany at

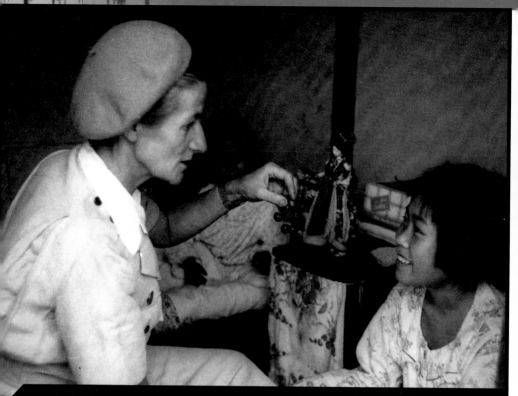

Marie Stopes, promoting birth control and family planning in Asia in the 1950s. Hulton Archive/Getty Images

the University of Manchester. She specialized in fossil plants and the problems of coal mining.

Stopes married her first husband, a botanist named Reginald Ruggles Gates, in 1911. She would later assert that her marriage was unconsummated and that she knew little about sex when she first married. Her failed marriage and its eventual end in 1916 played a large role in determining her future career, causing her to turn her attention to the issues of sex, marriage, and childbirth and their meaning in society.

Stopes initially saw birth control as an aid to marriage fulfillment and a means to save women from the physical strain of excessive childbearing. In this regard for quality of life of the individual woman, she differed from most other early leaders of the birth control movement, who were more concerned with social good, such as the elimination of overpopulation and poverty.

In 1918, Stopes married Humphrey Verdon Roe, cofounder of the A.V. Roe aircraft firm, who also had strong interests in the birth control movement. He helped her in the crusade that she then began. Their original birth control clinic—designed to educate women about the few methods of birth control available to them—was founded three years later, in the working-class Holloway district of London. That same year she became founder and president of the Society for Constructive Birth Control, a platform from which she spoke widely about the benefits of married women having healthy, desired babies.

Stopes is the author of *Married Love* and *Wise Parenthood* (both 1918), which were widely translated. When it first appeared her *Contraception: Its Theory, History and Practice* (1923) was the most comprehensive treatment of the subject.

After World War II, Stopes concentrated on promoting birth control in East Asian countries. She died on Oct. 2, 1958, at Dorking, Surrey, England, from breast cancer.

TERESA OF ÁVILA

(b. 1515–d. 1582)

Teresa of Ávila, also called Saint Teresa of Jesus, was one of the great mystics and religious women of the Roman Catholic Church and author of spiritual classics. She was the creator of the Carmelite Reform, which restored and stressed upon the severity and reflective character of primitive Carmelite life.

Teresa de Cepeda y Ahumada was born March 28, 1515, in Ávila, Spain. Her mother died in 1529, and, despite her father's opposition, Teresa entered the Carmelite Convent of the Incarnation at Ávila, probably in 1535. In 1558, Teresa began to consider restoring the Carmelite life to its original observance of severity, which had relaxed in the 14th and 15th centuries. In 1562, with Pope Pius IV's authorization, she opened the first convent (St. Joseph's) of the

Carmelite Reform. She insisted on poverty and subsistence only through charitable giving by the public.

In 1567, Teresa was directed to found more convents and establish monasteries. In the same year, while at Medina del Campo, Spain, she met a young Carmelite priest, Juan de Yepes (later St. John of the Cross, the poet and mystic), who she realized could initiate the Carmelite Reform for men. A year later, Juan opened the first monastery of the Primitive Rule at Duruelo, Spain.

Despite frail health and great difficulties, Teresa spent the rest of her life establishing and nurturing 16 more convents throughout Spain. Her frugal doctrine has been accepted as a classical exhibition of contemplative life, and her spiritual writings are among the most widely read. Her *Life of the Mother Teresa of Jesus* (1611) is autobiographical; the *Book of the Foundations* (1610) describes the establishment of her convents. Her writings on the progress of the Christian soul toward God are recognized masterpieces: *The Way of Perfection* (1583), *The Interior Castle* (1588), *Spiritual Relations, Exclamations of the Soul to God* (1588), and *Conceptions on the Love of God.* Of her poems, 31 are extant; of her letters, 458.

Teresa died on Oct. 4, 1582, in Alba de Tormes, Spain. She was canonized (made a saint) in 1622 by Pope Gregory XV, and was elevated to doctor of the church in 1970 by Pope Paul VI, the first woman to be so honored.

MARGARET THATCHER

(b. 1925–d. 2013)

The first woman to be elected prime minister of the United Kingdom, Margaret Thatcher was also the first woman to hold such a post in the history of Europe. The first prime minister since the 1820s to win three consecutive elections, Thatcher held office longer than any other 20th-century British leader.

Margaret Hilda Roberts was born on Oct. 13, 1925, at Grantham, Lincolnshire, England. She ran errands for the Conservative Party in the 1935 election and maintained this association as a member of the

Oxford University Conservative Association. A science graduate of Oxford, she worked as a research chemist.

Her first attempts to win a seat in Parliament were in 1950 and 1951. She lost both elections. In 1951, she married businessman Denis Thatcher. To equip herself for politics she began studying law, with an emphasis on taxation and patent policy. In 1959, Thatcher ran again for Parliament from a safe Conservative north London district and won. She served as secretary to the Ministry of Pensions and Insurance from 1961 to 1964 and as secretary of state for education and science in Edward Heath's Cabinet from 1970 to 1974. After the Conservative Party's loss of two general elections in 1974, she followed Heath as head of the party. When the Conservative Party won the 1979 elections, Thatcher became prime minister.

She belonged to the most conservative wing of her party, advocating cuts in taxation, an end to government controls, and reductions in public expenditures. Her early policies caused widespread unemployment and a number of business bankruptcies. A popular victory in the Falkland Islands conflict of 1982, however, led to a landslide victory in the 1983 elections. Her stature as a world leader increased when she visited the Soviet Union in March 1987, less than three months before she won another remarkable victory.

Thatcher's declared objective was to "destroy socialism." Her "unfinished revolution" to reshape British political, economic, and social life—mainly through privatization—was labeled Thatcherism. Because of her strong leadership, she was called the Iron Lady. She supported the NATO alliance and the European Communities, though her opposition to "Europe 1992" integration adversely affected her popularity and helped lead to her resignation in November 1990.

Despite her official withdrawal from office, Thatcher continued to cast a shadow over world politics. She was especially outspoken in her opposition to Britain's participation in several institutions of the European Union, and she outlined her position in her book *Statecraft: Strategies for a Changing World* (2002). In 1991, she established the Margaret Thatcher Foundation, which promotes democracy and free markets, particularly in the formerly communist countries of Eastern and Central Europe. She was made a peeress for life in the House of Lords in 1992, and in 1995, Queen Elizabeth II conferred upon her the Order of the

The empress Theodora (third from left), *shown with her retinue, in a Byzantine mosaic adorning the Basilica of San Vitale in Ravenna, Italy.* mountainpix/Shutterstock.

Garter, the highest British civil and military honor. In March 2002, after suffering a series of minor strokes, Thatcher announced her retirement from public life. She died on April 8, 2013, in London.

THEODORA

(b. 497–d. 548)

T he Byzantine empress Theodora, wife of the emperor Justinian I, was probably the most powerful woman in Byzantine history. Her intelligence and political insight made her Justinian's most trusted adviser, enabling her to use the power and influence of her office to promote religious and social policies that favored her interests.

132

Little is known of Theodora's early life, but it is believed that she was born in *c.* 497. She became an actress while still young, leading an unconventional life that included giving birth to at least one child out of wedlock. For a time, she made her living as a wool spinner. Attracted by her beauty and intelligence, Justinian made her his mistress, raised her to the rank of patrician (upper-class), and in 525 married her. When Justinian succeeded to the throne in 527, she was proclaimed Augusta.

Theodora exercised considerable influence during Justinian's reign. Her name is mentioned in nearly all the laws passed during that period. She greeted representatives of foreign lands and corresponded with foreign rulers, functions usually reserved for the emperor. Her influence in political affairs was best illustrated in the Nika revolt of January 532. The two political factions in Constantinople, the Blues and the Greens, united in their opposition to the government and set up a rival emperor. Justinian's advisers urged him to flee, but Theodora advised him to stay and save his empire, whereupon Justinian's general, Belisarius, gathered the revolutionaries into one place and had them killed.

Theodora is remembered as one of the first rulers to recognize the rights of women. She passed strict laws aimed at prohibiting the sale of young girls into sexual slavery and altering the divorce laws to give greater benefits to women.

Theodora's death, possibly from cancer or gangrene, was a severe blow to Justinian. Her importance in Byzantine political life is shown by the fact that little significant legislation dates from the period between her death and that of Justinian (565).

SOJOURNER TRUTH

(b. 1797–d. 1883)

"Children, I talk to God and God talks to me!" This was the usual opening of abolitionist, or antislavery, speaker and civil rights pioneer Sojourner Truth.

Her given name was Isabella Van Wagener, and she was born a slave in Ulster County, N.Y., in about 1797.

The circumstances surrounding her liberation are uncertain, but her surname was taken from Isaac Van Wagener, who was reportedly the last of several masters and the man who freed her in 1827. She moved to New York City, where she worked as a domestic servant. There she became closely associated with a Christian evangelist named Elijah Pierson. In 1843, she left New York, took the name Sojourner Truth, and began a life of preaching that carried her throughout the Northern states. Her growing reputation and personal magnetism drew large crowds wherever she appeared. She supported herself by selling copies of *The Narrative of Sojourner Truth*, which she had dictated to a friend.

She was a powerful foe of slavery, and in the 1850s, she added the women's rights movement to her causes. During the Civil War she served as a counselor to freed slaves in Washington, D.C. Her later years were spent helping freed slaves and lecturing in the North. She died at her home in Battle Creek, Mich., on Nov. 26, 1883.

HARRIET TUBMAN

(b. 1820–d. 1913)

A runaway slave herself, Harriet Tubman helped so many others escape to freedom that she became known as the "Moses of her people." During the Civil War, she served the Union Army as a nurse, cook, scout, and spy.

Harriet Tubman was born Araminta Ross in about 1820 on a plantation near Bucktown, Md. She was one of 11 children of a slave couple. When she was seven, she was hired out to do housework and look after white children on nearby farms. Later she became a field hand. While still a teenager, she was struck on the head by an overseer. As a result of the blow, she fell asleep suddenly several times a day for the rest of her life. Hard work toughened her, and before she was 19 she was as strong as the men with whom she worked.

In 1844, Ross married a free black, John Tubman. She left him in 1849, when her fear of being sold farther south spurred her to escape. She traveled at night, aided by the Underground Railroad, a secret network of people who helped fugitive slaves reach the Northern states and Canada.

In Philadelphia, Pa., and later at Cape May, N.J., Tubman worked as a maid in hotels and clubs. By December 1850, she had saved enough money to make the first of 19 daring journeys back into the South to lead other slaves out of bondage. In 1851, she returned for her husband but found he had remarried.

Tubman worked closely with the Underground Railroad. Often she left fugitives in the care of other "conductors" after leading them part of the way herself. She maintained strict discipline during the perilous journeys to the North. If a runaway lagged behind or lost faith and wished to

Full-length portrait of Harriet Tubman, who was a woman with many titles: nurse, spy, and conductor on the Underground Railroad. Library of Congress Prints & Photographs Division

turn back, she forced him on at gunpoint. Before the Civil War, she freed her parents and most of her brothers and sisters as well as hundreds of other slaves.

Slave owners were constantly on the lookout for Tubman and offered large rewards for her capture, but they never succeeded in seizing her or any of the slaves she helped escape during her work for the Underground Railroad. Much later in life she proudly recalled: "I never ran my train off the track, and I never lost a passenger."

Tubman supported her parents and worked to raise money for her missions into the South. She spoke at abolitionist meetings and at women's rights assemblies, often concealing her name for protection from slave hunters. Her forceful leadership led the white abolitionist John Brown to refer to her admiringly as "General" Tubman. She helped

Brown plan his October 1859 raid on the federal arsenal at Harpers Ferry, W. Va., and promised that many of the slaves she had freed would join him. Only illness prevented her from fighting at Brown's side during the raid itself.

During the Civil War, Tubman served the Union Army. She nursed and cooked for white soldiers, for example, as well as for sick and starving blacks who sought protection behind Union lines. She acted as both a scout and a spy, often bravely leading Union raiding parties into Confederate territory. For this, she won the respect of many grateful Union officers. But her efforts went unrewarded. She spent many decades trying to collect $1,800 in back pay from the federal government, which refused to recognize her wartime services. When in 1899 she was finally granted a pension, it was given to her not for her own deeds but because she was the widow of Nelson Davis, a Civil War veteran whom she had married in 1869.

Tubman had settled in Auburn, N.Y., in 1857. After the Civil War she fed, sheltered, and nursed any blacks who came to her home for aid. Although she was in poor health, she worked to support two schools for freedmen in the South and continued to provide a home for her parents. She often had to borrow money for food from friends who gratefully remembered her heroic exploits in the fight against slavery. After many years of effort, she was able to sponsor a home for needy blacks in Auburn, which was opened in 1908.

Scenes in the Life of Harriet Tubman, her first biography, published in 1869, was written by Sarah Hopkins Bradford to raise money for her support. In subsequent editions, the title was changed to *Harriet Tubman: The Moses of Her People.* Harriet Tubman died in Auburn on March 10, 1913, and was buried with military honors. A year later the city unveiled a tablet in her memory.

VICTORIA

(b. 1819–d. 1901)

Queen Victoria was the long-reigning monarch of the United Kingdom and, later, empress of India. The last of the House of Hanover,

Victoria, queen of the United Kingdom of Great Britain and Ireland and empress of India. Hulton Archive/Getty Images

she gave her name to an era, the Victorian Age. During her reign the English monarchy took on its modern ceremonial character.

Alexandrina Victoria of the House of Hanover was born at Kensington Palace in London on May 24, 1819. Her father, the Duke of Kent, was the fourth son of George III. Her mother was a German princess.

Victoria was 18 years old when she became queen of the United Kingdom upon the death of her uncle William IV in 1837. She was crowned at Westminster Abbey on June 28, 1838. As a young regent she met and fell in love with her first cousin, Prince Albert of Saxe-Coburg-Gotha. They were married in 1840 after Victoria had decided that as queen it was her right to propose to Albert. The marriage was a happy one, despite Albert's difficulty adjusting to political life and his role in the royal court. The queen had insisted that he be given the title of prince consort, but the government and many of the people were critical. They objected to any part the prince took in advising the queen on affairs of state.

Victoria and Albert had nine children, whose marriages were arranged by the queen. Her eldest daughter became empress of Germany and mother of William II, and her granddaughter was the last empress of Russia. By the end of the 19th century, Victoria had so many royal relatives that she was called the "grandmother of Europe."

After Albert's untimely death in 1861, Victoria went into seclusion. She avoided London and spent most of her time at Balmoral Castle in Scotland, at Osborne House on the Isle of Wight, and at Windsor. The fall from power of Prime Minister Benjamin Disraeli, a favorite of Victoria's, in 1880 was a further blow to the queen. The self-isolated monarch became an almost legendary figure until the last years of her reign. The longest reign in British history (64 years), it was marked with the glitter and pageantry of her Golden Jubilee in 1887 and her Diamond Jubilee in 1897.

Victoria was fortunate through most of her reign in having a succession of politically able Cabinet ministers. She also happened to be queen of Great Britain for most of the 19th century—a period that saw more changes than any other that had come before. The queen became the living symbol of peace and prosperity, and she made the

Crown a symbol of "private virtue and public honor." Victoria died on the Isle of Wight on Jan. 22, 1901.

ÉLISABETH VIGÉE-LEBRUN

(b. 1755–d. 1842)

French painter Élisabeth Vigée-Lebrun was one of the most successful of all women artists. She painted portraits of European society figures and of royalty, and she is especially noted for her portraits of women.

Marie-Louise-Élisabeth Vigée was born on April 16, 1755, in Paris, France. Her father was Louis Vigée, a portrait artist who became her first teacher. In 1776, she married an art dealer, J.-B.-P. Lebrun. Her great opportunity came in 1779, when she was summoned to the Versailles palace to paint a portrait of Queen Marie-Antoinette. The two women became friends, and over the next decade Vigée-Lebrun painted more than 20 portraits of Marie-Antoinette in a great variety of poses and costumes. She also painted a great number of self-portraits, in the style of various artists whose work she admired. In 1783, because of her friendship with the queen, Vigée-Lebrun was grudgingly accepted into the Royal Academy.

When the French Revolution broke out in 1789, Vigée-Lebrun left France. For 12 years she traveled in Italy, Austria, Germany, and Russia, painting portraits and playing a leading role in society. She returned to Paris in 1801 but disliked social life there during Napoleon's era. Vigée-Lebrun soon left for London, England, where she painted pictures of the royal court and of British Romantic poet Lord Byron. Later she went to Switzerland, where she painted a portrait of popular French-Swiss intellectual Madame de Staël. About 1810, Vigée-Lebrun moved back to Paris, where she continued to paint until her death.

Vigée-Lebrun was one of the most technically masterful portraitists of her era. Her pictures are notable for their freshness, charm, and sensitivity. During her career, by her own count, she painted 900 pictures, including some 600 portraits and about 200 landscapes. Vigée-Lebrun was a woman of much wit and charm. Her memoirs, *Souvenirs de ma vie*

(1835–37; "Reminiscences of My Life"), are a lively account of her life and times. Vigée-Lebrun died on March 30, 1842, in Paris.

SIMONE WEIL

(b. 1909–d.1943)

Simone Weil was a French mystic, social philosopher and activist in the French Resistance during World War II, whose posthumously published works had particular influence on French and English social thought.

Weil was born on Feb. 3, 1909, in Paris, France. Intellectually precocious, Weil also expressed social awareness at an early age. At five she refused sugar because the French soldiers at the front during World War I had none, and at six she was quoting the French dramatic poet Jean Racine (1639–99). In addition to studies in philosophy, classical philology, and science, Weil continued to embark on new learning projects as the need arose. She taught philosophy in several girls' schools from 1931 to 1938 and often became involved in conflicts with school boards as a result of her social activism, which entailed picketing, refusing to eat more than those on relief, and writing for leftist journals.

To learn the psychological effects of heavy industrial labor, she took a job in 1934–35 in an auto factory, where she observed the spiritually deadening effect of machines on her fellow workers. In 1936, she joined an anarchist unit near Zaragoza, Spain, training for action in the Spanish Civil War, but after an accident in which she was badly scalded by boiling oil, she went to Portugal to recuperate. Soon thereafter Weil had the first of several mystical experiences, and she subsequently came to view her social concerns as "ersatz Divinity." After the German occupation of Paris during World War II, Weil moved to the south of France, where she worked as a farm servant. She escaped with her parents to the United States in 1942 but then went to London to work with the French Resistance. To identify herself with her French compatriots under German occupation, Weil refused to eat more than the official ration in occupied France. Malnutrition and overwork led to a physical collapse, and during her hospitalization she was found to have tuberculosis. She died in 1943 after a few months spent in a sanatorium.

Weil's writings, which were collected and published after her death, fill about 20 volumes. Her most important works are *La Pesanteur et la grâce* (1947; *Gravity and Grace*), a collection of religious essays and aphorisms; *L'Enracinement* (1949; *The Need for Roots*), an essay upon the obligations of the individual and the state; *Attente de Dieu* (1950; *Waiting for God*), a spiritual autobiography; *Oppression et Liberté* (1955; *Oppression and Liberty*), a collection of political and philosophical essays on war, factory work, language, and other topics; and three volumes of *Cahiers* (1951–56; *Notebooks*). Though born of Jewish parents, Weil eventually adopted a mystical theology that came very close to Roman Catholicism. A moral idealist committed to a vision of social justice, Weil in her writings explored her own religious life while also analyzing the individual's relation with the state and God, the spiritual shortcomings of modern industrial society, and the horrors of totalitarianism.

OPRAH WINFREY

(b. 1954–)

As one of the most successful women in entertainment, Oprah Winfrey's extraordinary accomplishments are amazing by any standards. Born into poverty in the South, she grew to preside over an empire valued at more than $100 million.

Oprah Gail Winfrey was born on Jan. 29, 1954, on a farm in Kosciusko, Mississippi, to Vernita Lee and Vernon Winfrey, who were not married. At first raised by her strict maternal grandmother, Oprah was sent to live with her mother and two half-brothers in Milwaukee, Wisc., when she was 6 years old. With her mother struggling to make ends meet, Oprah had little supervision and started getting into trouble. When her mother could no longer handle her, Oprah was sent to Nashville, Tennessee, to live with her father and his wife, Zelma.

Vernon Winfrey, a barber who became a city council member, was a strict disciplinarian, but he also encouraged his daughter to read and engaged her in discussions. He demanded that his daughter add five new words to her vocabulary before she could have dinner each day.

Oprah Winfrey, arriving at a Los Angeles theater for the premier of Lee Daniels' The Butler in 2013. Jason Merritt/Getty Images

Under her father's guidance, Oprah Winfrey blossomed as a student. At 16 she won an contest that guaranteed her full scholarship to the University of Tennessee. She also received an invitation to the White House Conference on Youth. At Tennessee State University, Winfrey entered and won several beauty contests. She was subsequently offered a position by the local CBS affiliate television station and became Nashville's first black female co-anchor while she was still in college.

After graduating in 1976, Winfrey accepted an offer from the ABC affiliate in Baltimore, Maryland. After a few years she wound up on an early-morning talk show in Baltimore. In 1984, Winfrey and her producer, Debra DiMaio, moved to Chicago to liven up the lackluster *A.M. Chicago* show, which had been dominated in the ratings by Phil Donahue's show for more than 15 years. Within months Winfrey's show passed Donahue's in the ratings. By 1985, the show was expanded and renamed *The Oprah Winfrey Show.* Winfrey attracted scores of viewers, primarily women, who were attracted to her combination of boldness and vulnerability.

Winfrey's break as an actress came when she was cast by producer Quincy Jones and director Steven Spielberg in the feature *The Color Purple* (1985). She received Golden Globe and Oscar nominations for her performance.

In 1986, Winfrey formed a production company, Harpo, Inc. (The name Harpo is her first name spelled backwards.) Syndication of her show earned her millions of dollars, making her, by the mid-1990s, the highest-paid woman in the country. She purchased the film rights to many works of literature by black women. In 1995, she signed a deal with ABC to produce six made-for-television movies. Her production of Toni Morrison's Pulitzer Prize–winning book *Beloved*, in which she starred, was released in 1998.

Winfrey broke new ground in 1996 by starting an on-air book club. Each book chosen quickly rose to the top of the best-seller charts; Winfrey's effect on the publishing industry was significant. She further expanded her presence in the publishing industry with the highly successful launch of *O, the Oprah Magazine* in 2000 and *O at Home* in 2004; the latter folded in 2008.

In 1998, Winfrey expanded her media entertainment empire when she cofounded Oxygen Media, which launched a cable television network for women. In 2006, the Oprah & Friends channel debuted on satellite radio. She brokered a partnership with Discovery Communications in 2008, through which the Oprah Winfrey Network (OWN) replaced the Discovery Health Channel in January 2011.

The last original episode of *The Oprah Winfrey Show* aired in May 2011. *Oprah's Next Chapter*, a weekly prime-time interview program on OWN, debuted in January 2012.

Winfrey engaged in numerous philanthropic activities, including the creation of Oprah's Angel Network, which sponsors charitable initiatives worldwide. In 2007, she opened a school for disadvantaged girls in South Africa. She became an outspoken crusader against child abuse and received many honors and awards from civic, philanthropic, and entertainment organizations. In 2010, she was named a Kennedy Center honoree, and the following year she received the Jean Hersholt Humanitarian Award from the Academy of Motion Picture Arts and Sciences.

SARAH WINNEMUCCA

(b. 1844–d. 1891)

A Native American teacher, translator, and lecturer, Sarah Winnemucca dedicated herself to improving the lives of her people, the Paiute. Her writings are valuable for their description of Paiute life and for their insights into the impact of white settlement.

Winnemucca was born in about 1844 near Humboldt Lake, Nev. Her original name was Thocmetony, meaning "shell flower." Some say she was the daughter of Old Winnemucca and the granddaughter of explorer John C. Frémont's guide Captain Truckee, both Northern Paiute chiefs. Sarah and her brothers and sisters joined their mother on a ranch in California with Truckee, where Sarah first spent time with white people. She and her sister Mary studied at St. Mary's Convent school in San Jose in 1860, but the Paiute students were expelled from the school when white parents objected to their presence.

Sarah Winnemucca worked as a domestic servant during the Paiute War. In 1866, during the Snake War, the military asked her to interpret for them. Because she found the Bureau of Indian Affairs to be less competent than the military in managing Indian issues, she agreed. She mediated between her people and white settlers and interpreted for Gen. Oliver Otis Howard in the 1878 Bannock War. Despite her influence, the Paiute were moved to the Yakama Reservation in Washington. In 1879, Sarah spoke against the Bureau of Indian Affairs in San Francisco, and the government brought her to the eastern United States to lecture about the plight of the Paiute people. To attract crowds, Winnemucca even dressed as an Indian princess. She wrote a book entitled *Life Among the Piutes, Their Wrongs and Claims*, which was edited by Mary Tyler Mann, the widow of Horace Mann, and published in 1883.

Sarah Winnemucca received many private donations and used them to open a school for Indian children near Lovelock, Nev. She operated the school for three years. Winnemucca died of tuberculosis at her sister's home in Henry's Lake, Idaho, in 1891.

MARY WOLLSTONECRAFT

(b. 1759–d. 1797)

An English writer and women's rights advocate, Mary Wollstone-craft argued for female political, economic, and legal equality. In her most important work, *A Vindication of the Rights of Woman* (1792), she calls for women and men to be educated equally.

Wollstonecraft was born on April 27, 1759, in London. She taught school and worked as a governess, jobs that helped form the views put forth in her *Thoughts on the Education of Daughters* (1787). In 1788, she became a translator for the London publisher James Johnson. There she published several of her works, including the novel *Mary: A Fiction* (1788).

A few years later her work on woman's place in society, *A Vindication of the Rights of Woman*, came out. In it she argues that educating girls to the same degree as boys would result in women who would be not only exceptional wives and mothers but also capable workers in many professions. The publication of this work caused considerable controversy but did not bring about any immediate reforms. Beginning in the 1840s, however, members of the American and European women's movements, including U.S. women's rights pioneers Elizabeth

Cady Stanton and Margaret Fuller, popularized some of the book's principles.

Wollstonecraft left England for Paris in 1792 to experience the French Revolution. There she lived with an American, Captain Gilbert Imlay, and in the spring of 1794 she gave birth to a daughter, Fanny. The following year, distraught that her relationship with Imlay had ended, she attempted suicide. Wollstonecraft subsequently returned to London to resume her work for Johnson. She also joined an influential radical group that included William Godwin, Thomas Paine, Thomas Holcroft, William Blake, and William Wordsworth. In 1796, she began an affair with Godwin and became pregnant, and on March 29, 1797, the two were married. The marriage was happy but brief. Wollstonecraft died in London on Sept. 10, 1797, 11 days after giving birth to her second daughter, Mary, who would eventually become the wife of poet Percy Bysshe Shelley and write the gothic novel *Frankenstein*.

British novelist Virginia Woolf. George C. Beresford/Hulton Archive/Getty Images

VIRGINIA WOOLF

(b. 1882–d. 1941)

English writer Virginia Woolf was best known as a novelist. She also wrote pioneering essays on artistic theory, literary history, women's writing, and the politics of power.

She was born Adeline Virginia Stephen in London on Jan. 25, 1882, and was educated by her father, Sir Leslie Stephen. After his death she set up housekeeping in

Gordon Square in the district of Bloomsbury in London. Beginning in about 1907, her home was frequently visited by the young intellectuals who later became known as the Bloomsbury Group, including economist John Maynard Keynes, biographer Lytton Strachey, and novelist E.M. Forster. Also present was political writer Leonard Woolf, who became her husband in 1912. The couple founded Hogarth Press as a publisher for Virginia Woolf's own books as well as those of other authors.

Woolf's first novels—*The Voyage Out* (1915) and *Night and Day* (1919)—were praised by the critics, but she was dissatisfied with them and began to experiment with stream-of-consciousness writing. This is a narrative technique in which the reader lives within the mind of the characters and watches the story unfold. Her first such work was *Jacob's Room* (1922), followed by *Mrs. Dalloway* (1925), *To the Lighthouse* (1927), and *The Waves* (1931). *Between the Acts* (1941) was her last novel.

Virginia Woolf was plagued by emotional problems for many years. During a period of disturbance, she drowned herself in Sussex on March 28, 1941. In the decades after her death, her long essay, *A Room of One's Own* (1929), became a major text of the feminist movement. In it she describes the difficulties encountered by women writers in a society dominated by males.

WUHOU

(b. 624–d. 705)

Wuhou rose to become empress of China during the Tang Dynasty (618–907). She ruled effectively for many years, the last 15 (690–705) in her own name. During her rule, she established a unified empire and brought about needed social changes that stabilized the dynasty, ushering in one of the most fruitful ages of Chinese civilization.

Wu Zhao was born in 624 CE. She entered the palace of the Tang emperor Taizong (ruled 626–649) in 638, at the age of 14, as a junior concubine (a woman who lives with a man but is not married to him). By that time, the Tang Dynasty had recently reunited China, largely through the efforts of Taizong. Upon Taizong's death in 649, she was sent to a Buddhist convent, as custom required. There the future empress Wuhou was visited by the new emperor, Gaozong, who had her brought back to the palace to be his own favorite concubine. She first eliminated her female rivals within the palace—the existing empress and leading concubines—and in 655 gained the position of empress for herself, eventually bearing Gaozong four sons and one daughter.

Many elder statesmen, who had served Taizong and still exercised great influence over the government, opposed her elevation to the position of empress, mainly because her family was not one of the great aristocratic clans. They also objected to the nature of her relationship with Gaozong, claiming it was incestuous. By 660, the empress had triumphed over all opponents, who had been dismissed, exiled, and, in many instances, executed. Even the emperor's uncle, the head of the great family of the Changsun, of imperial descent, was hounded to death, and his relatives were exiled or ruined.

Virtually supreme power was now exercised by the Wuhou empress in the name of the sickly Gaozong, who was often too ill to attend to state affairs for long periods. She governed the empire with great efficiency, employing able men who clearly felt loyalty to her and stood by her when she was challenged. Her great ability as an administrator, her courage, decisive character, and readiness to use ruthless means against any opponent, however highly placed, won her the respect, if not the love, of the court. In the years between 655 and 675, the Tang Empire conquered Korea under military leaders who were picked and promoted by the empress.

When Gaozong died in 683, he was succeeded by his son Li Xian (by Wuhou), known as the Zhongzong emperor. The new emperor had been married to a woman of the Wei family, who now sought to put herself in the same position of authority as that of Wuhou, for Zhongzong was as weak and incompetent as his father. After one month Wuhou deposed her son, exiled him, and installed as emperor her second son, Li Dan (the Ruizong emperor), whose authority was in name only. A revolt raised by Tang loyalists and ambitious young officials in the south was crushed within weeks, with the loyal cooperation of the main armies of the throne. This demonstration of the support she commanded in the public service made the position of the empress unshakable.

Six years later, in 690, at age 65, the empress usurped the throne itself.

Accepted without revolt, she ruled for 15 years, changing the name of the dynasty to Zhou. In 698, the exiled Zhongzong, an heir of the Tang family of Li, was recalled to court and made crown prince. It would appear that the empress seemed to have had no ambition on behalf of her own family, only a determination to retain power for herself to the end.

In the last years of her life, from 699, the empress gave her favor to the Zhang brothers, who engaged her affection by amusing and flattering her. As she gradually fell into ill health, she depended increasingly on the care of the Zhang brothers. In February 705, a conspiracy formed among the leading ministers and generals, who seized the palace, executed the Zhang brothers, and compelled the empress, old and ill, to yield power to Zhongzong, who reigned until 710.

Wuhou retired to another palace in Luoyang and died there on Dec. 16, 705.

ROSALYN S. YALOW

(b. 1921–d. 2011)

Yalow was an American medical physicist and joint recipient (with Andrew V. Schally and Roger Guillemin) of the 1977 Nobel Prize for Physiology or Medicine, awarded for her development of radioimmunoassay (RIA), an extremely sensitive technique for measuring minute quantities of biologically active substances.

Rosalyn S. Yalow was born on July 19, 1921 in New York. She graduated with honors from Hunter College of the City University of New York in 1941 and four years later received her Ph.D. in physics from the University of Illinois. From 1946 to 1950, she lectured on physics at Hunter, and in 1947, she became a consultant in nuclear physics to the Bronx Veterans Administration Hospital, where from 1950 to 1970 she was physicist and assistant chief of the radioisotope service.

With a colleague, the American physician Solomon A. Berson, Yalow began using radioactive isotopes to examine and diagnose various disease conditions. Yalow and Berson's investigations into the mechanism underlying type II diabetes led to their development of RIA. In the 1950s, it was known that individuals treated with injections of animal insulin developed resistance to the hormone and so required greater amounts of it to offset the effects of the disease; however, a satisfactory explanation for this phenomenon had not been put forth. Yalow and Berson theorized that the foreign insulin stimulated the production of antibodies, which became bound to the insulin and prevented the hormone from entering cells and carrying out its function of metabolizing glucose. In order to prove their hypothesis to a skeptical scientific community, the researchers combined techniques from immunology and radioisotope tracing to measure minute amounts of these antibodies, and the RIA was born. It was soon apparent that this method could be used to measure hundreds of other biologically active substances, such as viruses, drugs, and other proteins. This made possible such practical applications as the screening of blood in blood banks for hepatitis virus and the determination of effective dosage levels of drugs and antibiotics.

In 1970, Yalow was appointed chief of the laboratory later renamed the Nuclear Medical Service at the Veterans Administration Hospital. In 1976, she was the first female recipient of the Albert Lasker Basic Medical Research Award. Yalow became a distinguished professor at large at the Albert Einstein College of Medicine at Yeshiva University in 1979 and left in 1985 to accept the position of Solomon A. Berson Distinguished Professor at Large at the Mount Sinai School of Medicine. She was awarded the National Medal of Science in 1988.

GLOSSARY

ALLEGORY A tale in which ideas and principles are represented by fictional characters or events.

ANNEX To attach as a quality, consequence, or condition.

CLANDESTINE Marked by, held in, or conducted with secrecy.

CONCUBINE A woman with whom a man cohabits without being married.

EVANGELIZE To preach or speak out convincingly, in an attempt to convert others to a certain way of behaving or thinking.

EXPATRIATE To withdraw oneself from residence in or allegiance to one's native country.

INDIGENOUS Produced, growing, living, or occurring naturally in a particular region or environment.

NEUROSIS A mental and emotional disorder marked by various physical, physiological, and mental disturbances such as anxieties, or phobias.

PROPAGANDA The spreading of ideas, information, or rumor for the purpose of helping or injuring an institution, a cause, or a person.

REGENT A person who governs a kingdom when a king or queen is unable to rule because of age or absence.

SUFFRAGE The legal right to vote.

VEHEMENT Marked by forceful energy.

FOR MORE INFORMATION

Canadian Committee on Women's History
Canadian Historical Association
1201-130, Albert Street
Ottawa, ON K1P 5G4
Canada
(613) 233-7885
Web site: http://www.chashcacommittees-comitesa.ca
Affiliated with the Canadian Historical Association, the Canadian
    Committee on Women's history seeks to promote teaching and
    research in the field of women's history. The group offers research,
    publications, meetings, conferences, and academic networking op-
    portunities toward that end.

National Women's Hall of Fame
76 Fall Street
Seneca Falls, NY 13148
(315) 568-8060
Web site: http://www.greatwomen.org
Created in 1969, the National Women's Hall of Fame is a nonprofit
    organization centering on the achievements of remarkable wom-
    en in the United States. In addition to its on-site exhibit of hall
    inductees and an online searchable database, the organization of-
    fers a members newsletter, a research center, and various special
    events.

National Women's History Museum
205 S. Whiting Street Suite 254
Alexandria, VA 22304
(703) 461-1920
Founded in 1996, the National Women's History Museum researches,
    collects, and exhibits the contributions of women to the social, cul-
    tural, economic and political life of the United States in a context
    of world history. The organization offers educational programs,

scholarship and research opportunities, and an online museum.

National Women's History Project

730 2nd Street, No. 469

P.O. Box 469

Santa Rosa, CA 95402

(707) 636-2909

Web site: http://www.nwhp.org

For more than 30 years, the National Women's History Project has
been a substantial resource for information and material about
the unfolding roles of women in American history. Activities and
events conducted by the group include workshops, conferences,
discussion groups, and oversight of National Women's History
Month throughout the United States.

Honoring Eleanor Roosevelt

The Roosevelt-Vanderbilt National Historic Site

4097 Albany Post Road

Hyde Park, NY 12538

(845) 516-4413

Web site: http://www.honoringeleanorroosevelt.org

Honoring Eleanor Roosevelt is a public-private partnership between
the National Park Service and the National Trust for Historic
Preservation and was founded by Hillary Clinton as a priority
project of Save America's Treasures.

WEB SITES

Due to the changing nature of Internet links, Rosen Publishing has
developed an online list of Web sites related to the subject of this book.
This site is updated regularly. Please use this link to access the list:

http://www.rosenlinks.com/pysk/women

FOR FURTHER READING

Adams, Simon. *Elizabeth I: The Outcast Who Became Englands' Queen*. Washington, D.C.: National Geographic Children's Books, 2008.

Beilenson, Eveylyn, and Lois Kaufman. *Women Who Dared*. White Plains, NY: Peter Pauper Press, 2009.

Fleming, Candice. *Amelia Lost: The Life and Disappearance of Amelia Earhart*. New York, NY: Schwartz & Wade, 2011

Krull, Kathleen. *Lives of Extraordinary Women: Rulers, Rebels, and What the Neighbors Thought*. New York, NY: Harcourt, 2013.

Maasburg, Leo. *Mother Teresa of Calcutta: A Personal Portrait*. San Fransisco, CA: Ignatius Press, 2010

Nagle, Jeanne. *Oprah Winfrey: Profile of a Media Mogul*. New York, NY: Rosen Publishing, 2007.

Pavlova, Anna. *I Dreamed I Was a Ballerina*. New York, NY; Antheneum Books for Young Readers, 2001.

Steele, Philip. *Marie Curie: The Woman Who Changed the Course of Science*. Washington, D.C.; National Geographic Children's Books, 2008.

Waisman, Charlotte S., and Jill S. Tietjen. *Her Story: A Timeline of Women Who Changed America*. New York, NY: HarperCollins, 2008.

INDEX

A

abolitionist movement, 3, 14, 133, 135
abortion, 106, 119
Academy of Motion Picture Arts and Sciences, 144
Accumulation of Capital, The, 81–82
Addams, Jane, 1–3
African National Congress, 58
AIDS, 17, 37, 83
Albert Lasker Basic Medical Research Award, 105, 150
Alcestis, 59
Alito, Samuel A., Jr., 106
American Birth Control League, 120
American Civil War, 15, 40, 134, 135, 136
American Foundation for the Blind, 76
Anderson, Marian, 117
Anderson, Sherwood, 123, 124
Anne Frank Foundation, 54
Anne Frank House, 54
Anthony, Susan B., 3–4
Antony, Mark, 28, 29
apartheid, 58
Appalachian Spring, 59
Arkansas Advocates for Children and Families, 30
Arnaz, Desi, 9
Association for Support of Children's Rights, 45
Aung San Suu Kyi, 4–6
Austen, Jane, 6–7
Autobiography of Alice B. Toklas, The, 124

B

Ball, Lucille, 7–9
Bandaranaike, Sirimavo R.D., 10–11
Bandaranaike, S.W.R.D., 10
Bath, The, 19
Battle of the Sexes, 77, 79
Becquerel, Henri, 32
Bell, Alexander Graham, 76
Bell, Gertrude, 11–12
Beloved, 143
Bernard, Julie, 12
Bernhardt, Sarah, 12–14
Berson, Solomon A., 149, 150
Big Street, The, 9
birth control, 56, 119, 120, 125, 127, 128, 129
Blackwell, Elizabeth, 14–15
Blake, William, 146
Blond Venus, 39
Blood Money, 7
Bloomsbury Group, 147
Blue Angel, The, 38
Blunt, Lady Anne, 12
Boleyn, Anne, 47, 90, 91
Booker Prize, 58
Book of the Foundations, 130
Bowes-Lyon, Elizabeth, 49
Boxer Rebellion, 27
Bradford, Sarah Hopkins, 136
Braque, Georges, 124
Bridgman, Laura, 75
Brontë sisters, 15–17
Brown, John, 135, 136
Brundtland, Gro Harlem, 17–18
Bureau of Indian Affairs, 144, 145
Burger's Daughter, 59
Burgos-Debray, Elisabeth, 94
Butler, Nicholas Murray, 2

C

Cannon, Annie Jump, 18–19
Caravaggio, 57